CURIOUS FEATURES OF EXTRAORDINARY CREATURES

NATURE'S CLEANUP CREW

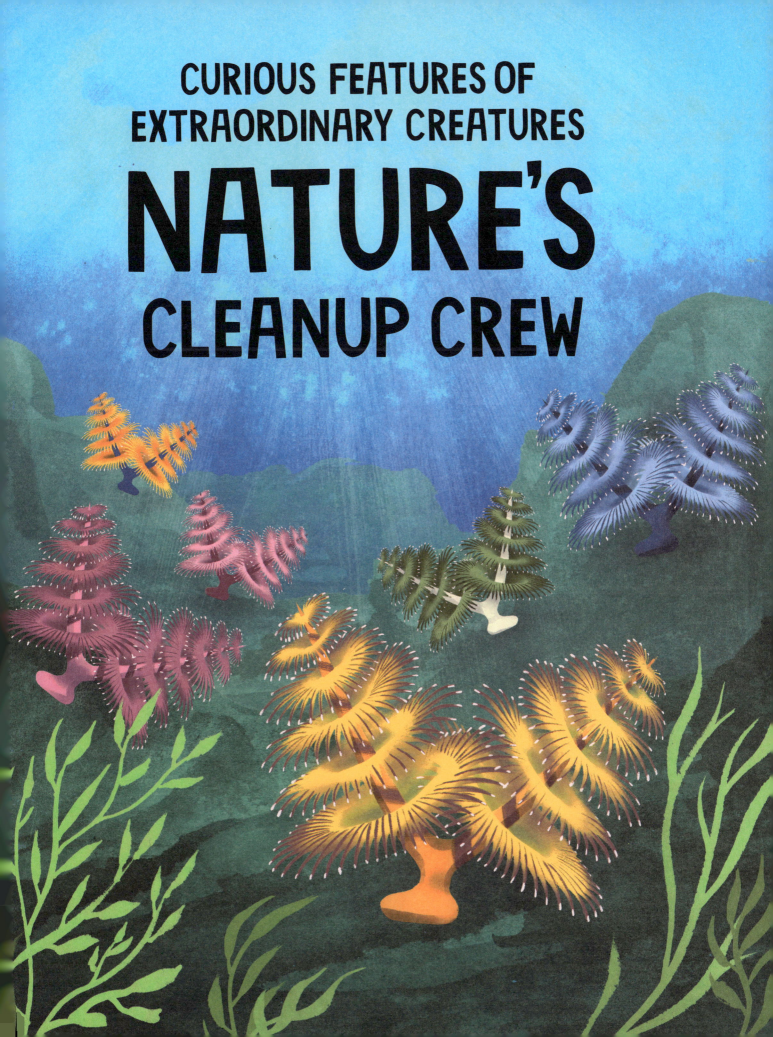

CURIOUS FEATURES OF EXTRAORDINARY CREATURES

NATURE'S CLEANUP CREW

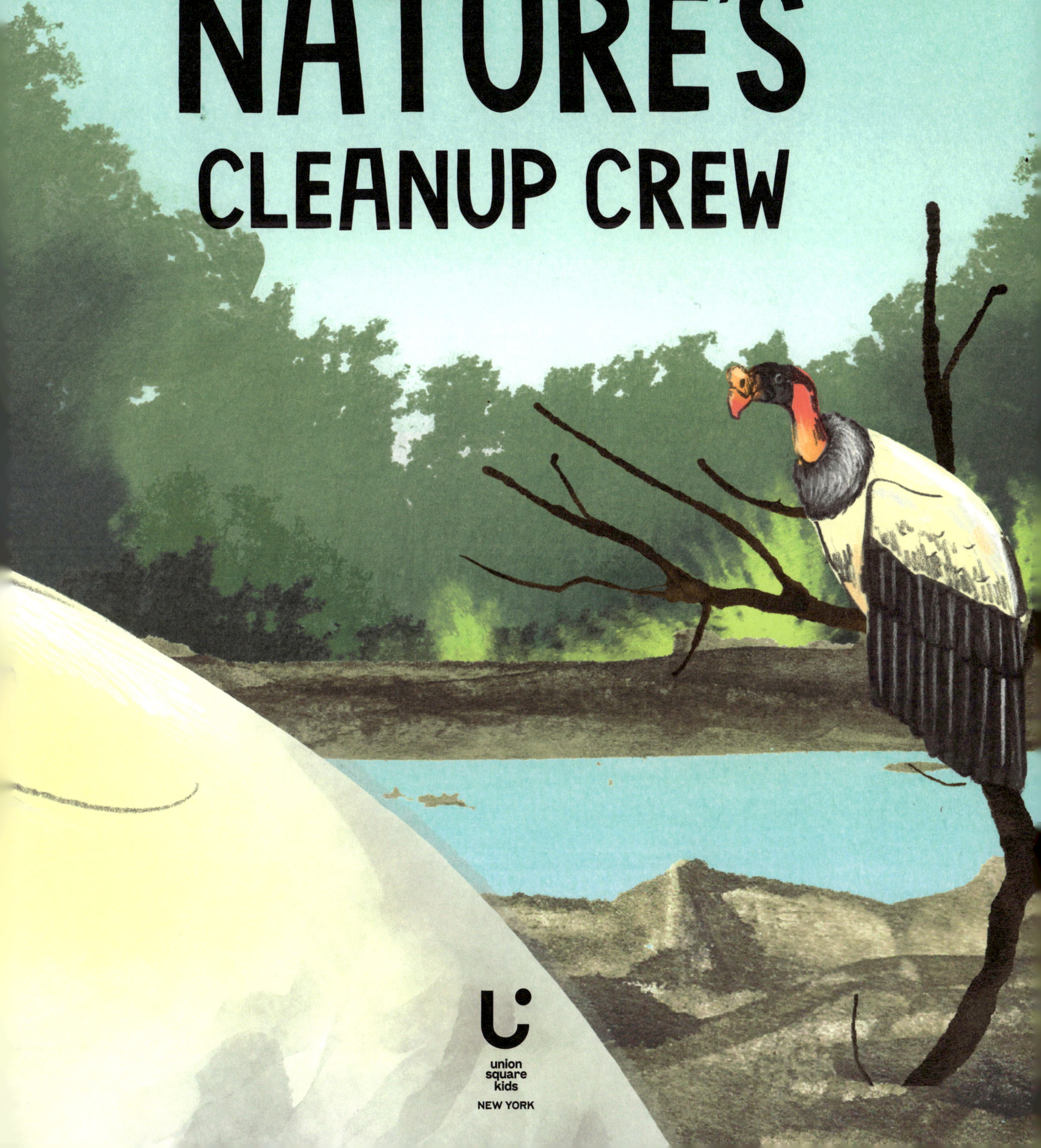

union square kids
NEW YORK

For mom–whose love and support means the world–FF

For Leonora and Etta–two of my favorite extraordinary creatures–CdlB

union square kids
NEW YORK

UNION SQUARE KIDS and the distinctive Union Square Kids logo are trademarks of Union Square & Co., LLC.

Union Square & Co., LLC, is a subsidiary of Sterling Publishing Co., Inc.

First published in 2025 in the United States and Canada by Union Square Kids, an imprint of Union Square & Co., LLC.
First published in 2025 in the United Kingdom by Kingfisher, an imprint of Macmillan Children's Books, London.

ISBN 978-1-4549-5943-4

For information about custom editions, special sales, and premium purchases, please contact specialsales@unionsquareandco.com.

Printed in China

Lot #:
2 4 6 8 10 9 7 5 3 1

12/24

unionsquareandco.com

Illustrator and concept: Fiona Fogg
Editor and consultant: Camilla de la Bedoyere
Senior designer: Lisa Sodeau, Jim Green
Editorial director: Elizabeth Yeates

FSC www.fsc.org MIX Paper | Supporting responsible forestry FSC® C116313

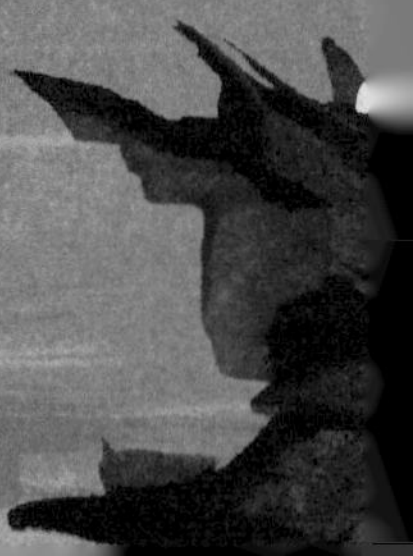

Contents

Introduction

This book showcases some of nature's most extraordinary stories. Dig and delve into dark and deep places to discover how the members of nature's cleanup crew keep our world healthy and its ecosystems in balance.

Rotting plants, dead animals, food waste, and piles of poop may be just types of garbage to us, but they are a marvelous source of food for a bustling army of busy recyclers. Whether they are animals, fungi, or microorganisms, these clever creatures use a range of super skills and nifty tricks to turn trash into treasure.

This book celebrates the standout contributions of some of the world's most impressive cleaners, from hungry hyenas that munch and crunch their way through bones, to sausage-like sea cucumbers that sweep up messes on the seabed, and pooper-scooper beetles.

Nature's cleanup crew doesn't just tidy up waste, they do magic with it! All types of waste contain materials, chemicals, or nutrients that can be turned into something new. When the cleanup crew gets to work, they release these special ingredients so the waste can be used again by living things to grow. That helps keep our precious planet healthy.

And you can help, too! As you explore *Curious Features of Extraordinary Creatures: Nature's Cleanup Crew,* think about your own impact on the natural world. Are you responsible for adding unnecessary waste to landfill sites? Challenge yourself to join the cleanup crew and do your best to recycle, reuse, and reduce the waste you create. It's an easy way to make the world a better place!

The Energy Cycle

Heat and light energy from the sun fuel almost all life on Earth. Plants use the energy in sunlight to make their own food. This energy transfers from plants to animals, microbes, and fungi when they eat, or digest, the plants.

The Food Chain

The way energy moves from plants to animals is called a food chain. The cleanup crew recycles energy back into the chain, creating an energy cycle. Around and around it goes!

Plants are called producers: they make food using the sun's energy, water, air, and nutrients from the soil.

Predators such as eagles eat snakes.
Snakes eat birds and frogs.
Consumers such as birds and frogs eat insects.
Insects eat plants.
Plants use the nutrients and the sun's energy to make food.
The eagle dies.
Decomposers turn the eagle's decaying body into nutrients.

In this food chain, waste is produced by all the organisms as they live and as they die. This is where our cleanup teams come in, clearing away dead plants, animals, and poop (feces).

They break organic matter into smaller particles, including nutrients that go back into the soil. This process is called decomposition, and it is an essential part of the energy cycle.

Cleanup Teams

Nature's cleanup crews have the super important job of breaking down dead plants and animals and turning them back into soil that helps new plants grow. They are nature's recycling team, making sure nothing goes to waste. Here are some of them:

Scavengers

Scavengers are animals that eat carrion—the remains of dead animals that they find. Scavengers can be small or large, but they often need the right tools to rip flesh, scales, and skin, such as claws, pincers, or teeth.

Detritivores

Small pieces of dead plant or animal remains are called detritus, and animals that eat them are called detritivores. Rarely picky, these creatures munch through almost any type of organic matter they find.

Decomposers produce a special liquid to break everything down even more.

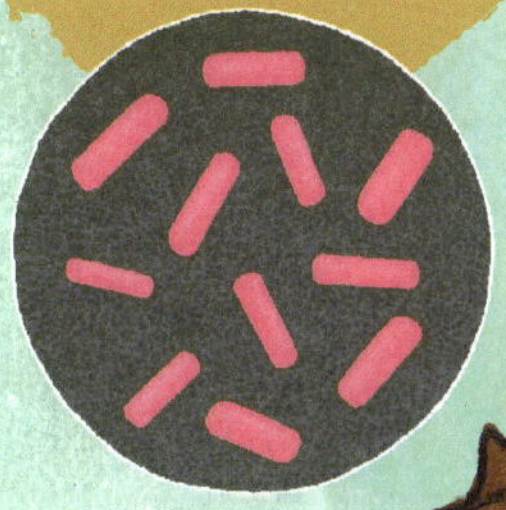

Decomposers

When an animal or plant is further broken up into its smallest parts, it is being decomposed. This important job is often carried out by the smallest members of the cleanup crew, such as microscopic animals, fungi, and bacteria.

The Safari Cleanup Crew

In the African savanna lives the majestic elephant. During its long life, it makes an enormous impact on the landscape, changing and creating habitats for millions of animals. When it dies, an elephant's body continues with this essential work—becoming food for other creatures and returning goodness to the soil.

Soaring overhead, vultures spot the dead elephant lying on the grass.
Using **large, powerful beaks**, they begin to pick at soft parts of the body. They struggle to break through the tough, leathery skin.
Spotted hyenas arrive. Their jaws are **immensely strong**, and they quickly start ripping open the carcass.
The vultures stand back while the **hyenas munch and crunch**. They are waiting their turn.
Attracted by the sights, smells, and sounds of the feast, **curious lions and leopards** come to investigate.
Day and night, the **carrion eaters squabble over the carcass**, devouring as much as they can.
The animals must act quickly as the body continues to break down.

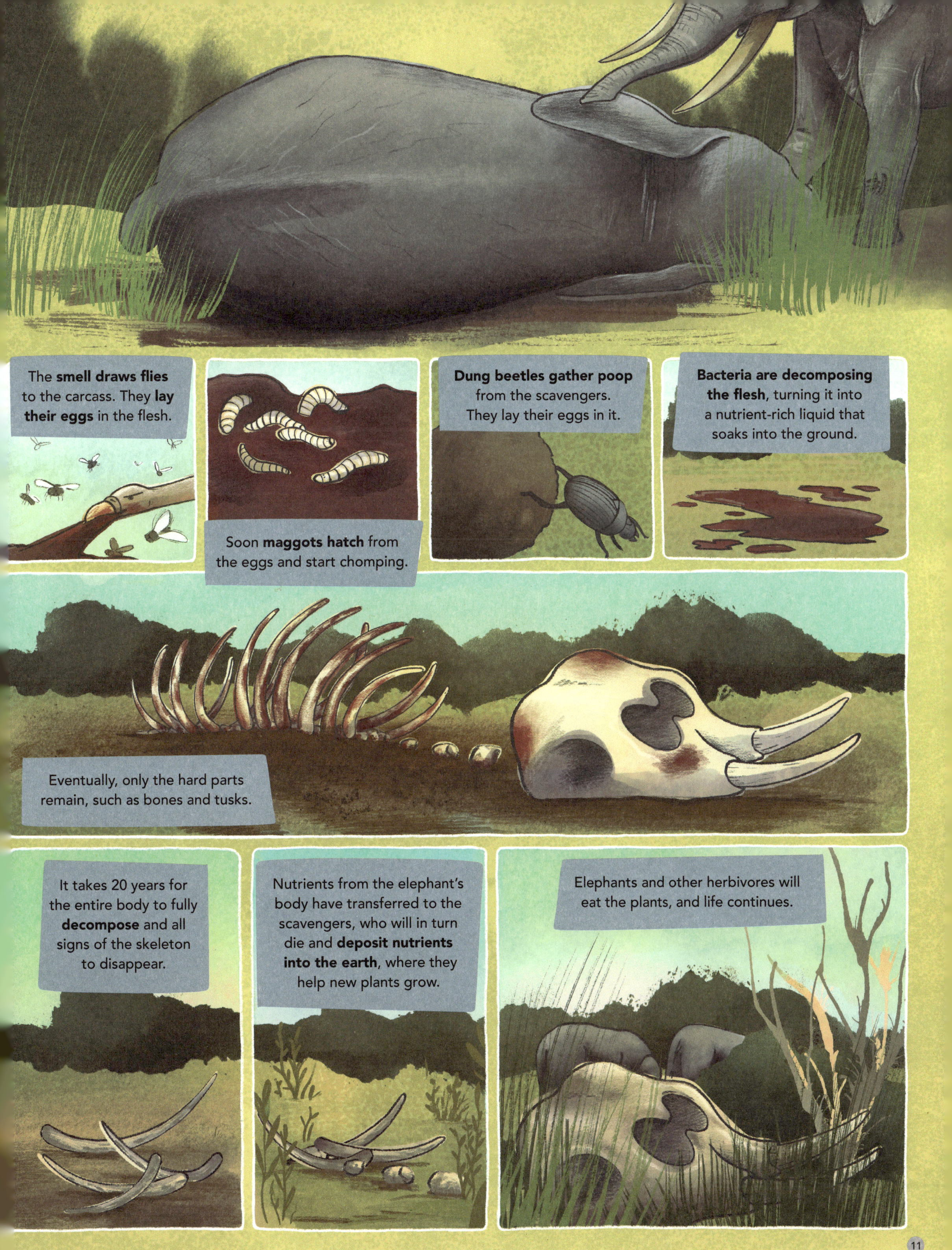

The **smell draws flies** to the carcass. They **lay their eggs** in the flesh.
Soon **maggots hatch** from the eggs and start chomping.
Dung beetles gather poop from the scavengers. They lay their eggs in it.
Bacteria are decomposing the flesh, turning it into a nutrient-rich liquid that soaks into the ground.
Eventually, only the hard parts remain, such as bones and tusks.
It takes 20 years for the entire body to fully **decompose** and all signs of the skeleton to disappear.
Nutrients from the elephant's body have transferred to the scavengers, who will in turn die and **deposit nutrients into the earth**, where they help new plants grow.
Elephants and other herbivores will eat the plants, and life continues.

Virginia Opossum

A clever scavenger that plays dead

These small nocturnal animals make the most of everything life throws at them—perhaps because they rarely live for longer than two years. They will make a home almost anywhere and eat almost anything, including carrion and garbage.

Virginia Opossum Fact File

Latin name:	***Didelphis virginiana***
Origin:	**North and Central America**
Habitat:	**Forests, woodlands, grasslands, parks, and yards**
Size:	**13–20 in. (33–50 cm) long**
Lifespan:	**2 years**
Diet:	**Small mammals, birds, insects, plants, carrion, and garbage**
Predators:	**Foxes, dogs, coyotes, raccoons, bobcats, owls, snakes, and humans**
Curiosity:	**A newborn Virginia opossum is about the size of a honeybee.**

A Virginia opossum relies on its superb senses—especially smell and sight—to find food in the dark. Its night vision is better than a cat's.

Opossums thrive in human habitats. They make dens in sheds and raid garbage cans for snacks.

A female gives birth to as many as 25 babies at a time, but she only has 13 teats to feed them, and they don't all survive.
Opossums are marsupials. This means the mother keeps the tiny babies in a pouch until they have grown bigger, when they ride around on her back!

Sometimes an opossum **pretends to be dead** when it comes under attack.
It curls up, **limp and motionless**, with its eyes open and jaw hanging slack.
If that doesn't work, the opossum releases **a foul-smelling scent**.
It can play dead for up to six hours, until the threat has gone.

Tasmanian Devil

A ferocious animal that quickly loses its temper but not its appetite

Tasmanian devils are famous for their fierce tempers and awesome, bone-crushing jaws. They lived on the Australian mainland until humans hunted them to extinction. Now found only in Tasmania, these fearless marsupials face a new threat to their survival.

The sun goes down, and Tasmanian devils **stir from their sleep**.
The delicious smell of rotting meat hangs in the air. It's time for the devils to start **following their noses**!
Roadkill is a popular source of food for Tasmanian devils.
They begin to gather at the side of the road where an animal has died. The **scavengers dig in**!
The devils' dinnertime is a raucous affair! They **screech, snarl, growl, sniff, and scream** as they compete for food.
A Tasmanian devil uses these noises to tell the others to back off. If it's loud enough, the **other devils may get scared and move away**.
Post-dinner slump!

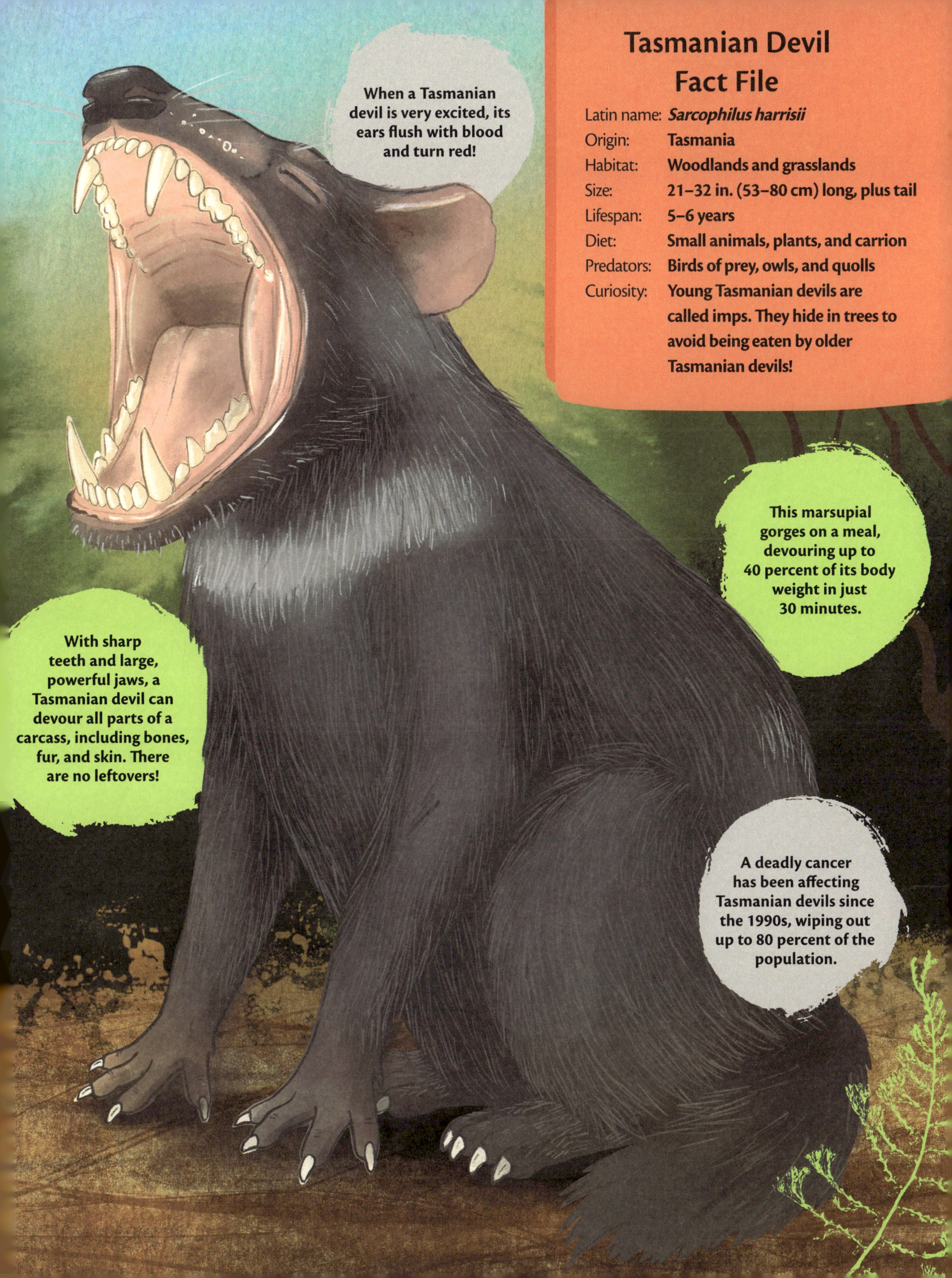

Tasmanian Devil Fact File

Latin name:	***Sarcophilus harrisii***
Origin:	**Tasmania**
Habitat:	**Woodlands and grasslands**
Size:	**21–32 in. (53–80 cm) long, plus tail**
Lifespan:	**5–6 years**
Diet:	**Small animals, plants, and carrion**
Predators:	**Birds of prey, owls, and quolls**
Curiosity:	**Young Tasmanian devils are called imps. They hide in trees to avoid being eaten by older Tasmanian devils!**

When a Tasmanian devil is very excited, its ears flush with blood and turn red!

This marsupial gorges on a meal, devouring up to 40 percent of its body weight in just 30 minutes.

With sharp teeth and large, powerful jaws, a Tasmanian devil can devour all parts of a carcass, including bones, fur, and skin. There are no leftovers!

A deadly cancer has been affecting Tasmanian devils since the 1990s, wiping out up to 80 percent of the population.

Striped Hyena

For hyenas, blood is thicker than water

Lurking in the shadows, this scavenger is rarely seen or heard. Secretive and shy, striped hyenas spend much of their lives alone, feasting on carrion at night. Then, at breeding time, families get together to share in the task of looking after cubs.

Striped Hyena Fact File

Latin name: ***Hyaena hyaena***
Origin: **Parts of Africa and Asia**
Habitat: **Grasslands, woodlands, and scrubland**
Size: **3 ft. (1 m) long**
Lifespan: **Up to 12 years**
Diet: **Carrion, small animals, and fruit**
Predators: **Humans**
Curiosity: **In some African villages, people leave their garbage outside for striped hyenas to clean up.**

Like many scavengers, this animal has an incredible sense of smell. Hyenas greet by sniffing each other's noses and rears!

Superstrong jaws are powerful enough to crunch through bones and hooves.

A scared hyena raises the thick mane of dark fur that runs from its head to its tail. This makes it look larger and more threatening.

A mother **gives birth to her pups in a den**. The pups' grandmothers and older sisters soon arrive to help out.

The **family shares the work** of caring for the pups, playing with them and guarding the den.

The **helpers bring back food** for the pups to feast on.

The helpers leave when the cubs are about one year old. Their work is done!

A group of hyenas is called a clan. Clans are led by female hyenas.
Hyenas have no natural predators, but they are sometimes hunted by humans.

King Vulture

A huge bird that is bold and quiet, and a king

With enormous black-and-white wings and fleshy skin on its head and neck, the king vulture is a gentle creature—it's happy to live alongside other species and is rarely agressive.

Like most other vultures, the king vulture does not have a voice box, which means it can only croak, squeal, grunt, and hiss.

The **king vulture flies up high**, keeping a watchful eye out.
It has almost **no sense of smell**, so it follows other scavengers to carrion sites.
King vultures are usually the last large scavengers to arrive at a carcass.
The smaller scavengers stand aside to let the powerful king vulture rip open the carcass.

As it ages, a king vulture's fleshy "nose" turns more orange. This tells other scavengers that this is truly the king of the carcass!

A female king vulture is not ready to breed until she is four or five years old. She lays just one egg at a time.

King vulture chicks are sooty black all over. It takes up to five years to grow the vibrant, folded, and fleshy skin on their heads and necks.

King Vulture Fact File

Latin name:	***Sarcoramphus papa***
Origin:	**Mexico, Central and South America**
Habitat:	**Mostly forests, but also grasslands**
Size:	**31 in. (80 cm) long, with a wingspan of 59 in. (1.5 m)**
Lifespan:	**Up to 25 years**
Diet:	**Carrion**
Predators:	**Humans**
Curiosity:	**These birds bow and bob their heads to impress their mates with the splendid colors of their skin.**

Sailors call this albatross and its close relatives "mollymawks."

Black-Browed Albatross Fact File

Latin name: ***Thalassarche melanophris***
Origin: **Oceans and coasts south of the equator**
Habitat: **Oceans and seas, rocky slopes and islands**
Size: **35 in. (90 cm) long**
Lifespan: **Up to 70 years**
Diet: **Fish and invertebrates**
Predators: **Rats, cats, and birds, including condors, turkey vultures, and skuas**
Curiosity: **This bird has a huge wingspan of up to 95 in. (240 cm).**

Black-Browed Albatross

Long-distance travelers in search of fast food and on-the-go treats

These albatrosses evolved to feed on fish, crustaceans, squid, and octopuses. However, they know that if they follow behind a fishing boat, they can swoop down to scavenge snacks from any waste that the boat leaves behind. It's a smart trick, but there can be a heavy price to pay.

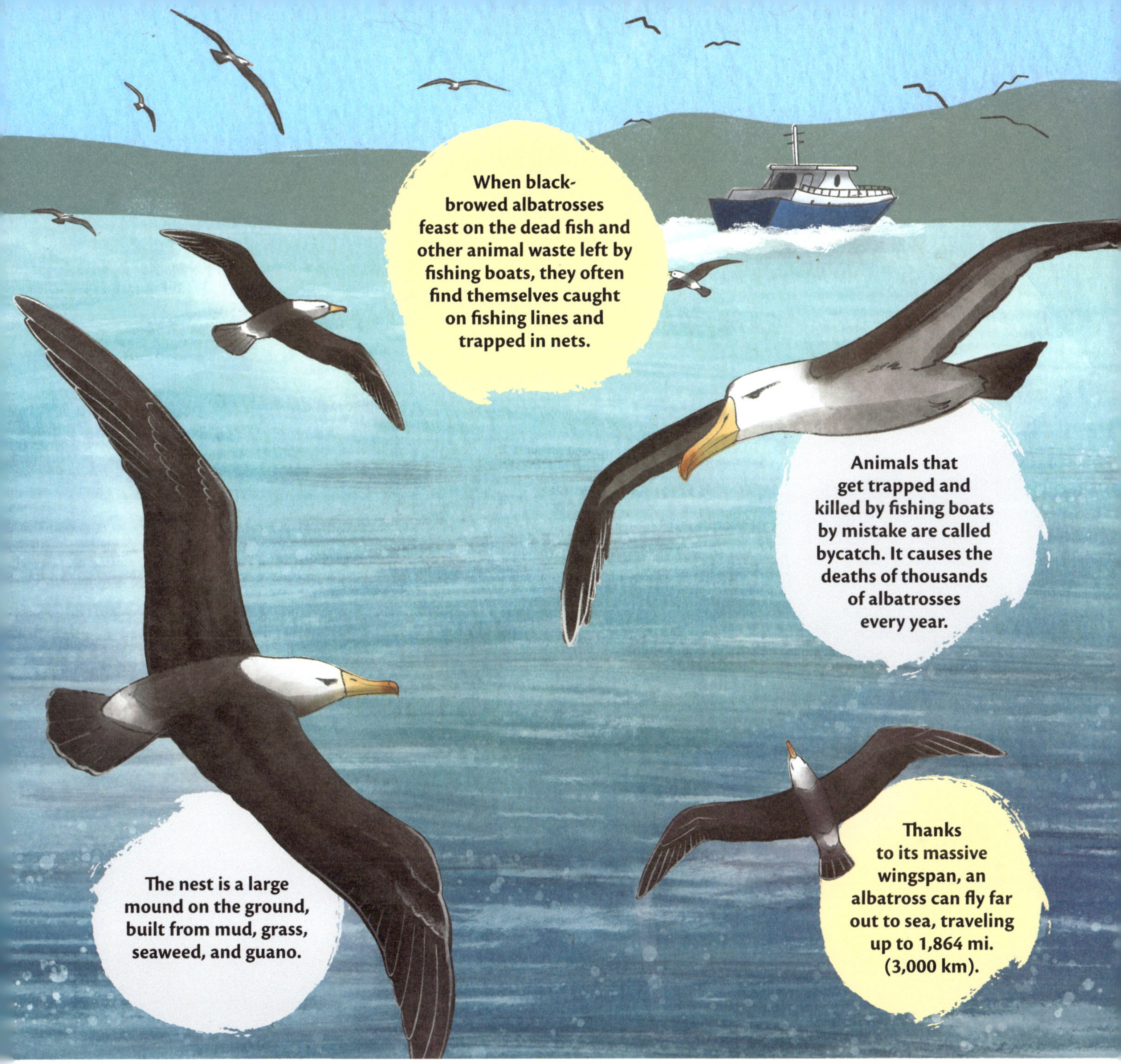

When black-browed albatrosses feast on the dead fish and other animal waste left by fishing boats, they often find themselves caught on fishing lines and trapped in nets.

Animals that get trapped and killed by fishing boats by mistake are called bycatch. It causes the deaths of thousands of albatrosses every year.

The nest is a large mound on the ground, built from mud, grass, seaweed, and guano.

Thanks to its massive wingspan, an albatross can fly far out to sea, traveling up to 1,864 mi. (3,000 km).

A black-browed albatross finds a partner, and **they mate for life**. Every year the birds return to the same nest and raise a chick.

The female bird lays a **single egg** on the bowl-shaped top of the nest.

The parents take turns **incubating their egg** until it hatches. They also share the job of feeding the chick.

When it is about **four months** old, the chick has grown its adult plumage. It is **ready to leave the nest** and fend for itself.

Marabou Stork

A wetland bird turned city street cleaner

With hunched shoulders; dark, cape-like wings; and black, beady eyes, this big, eerie bird is an impressive sight. The marabou stork is often found in wetlands, near where humans live. It eats carrion and scavenges for garbage in city dumps.

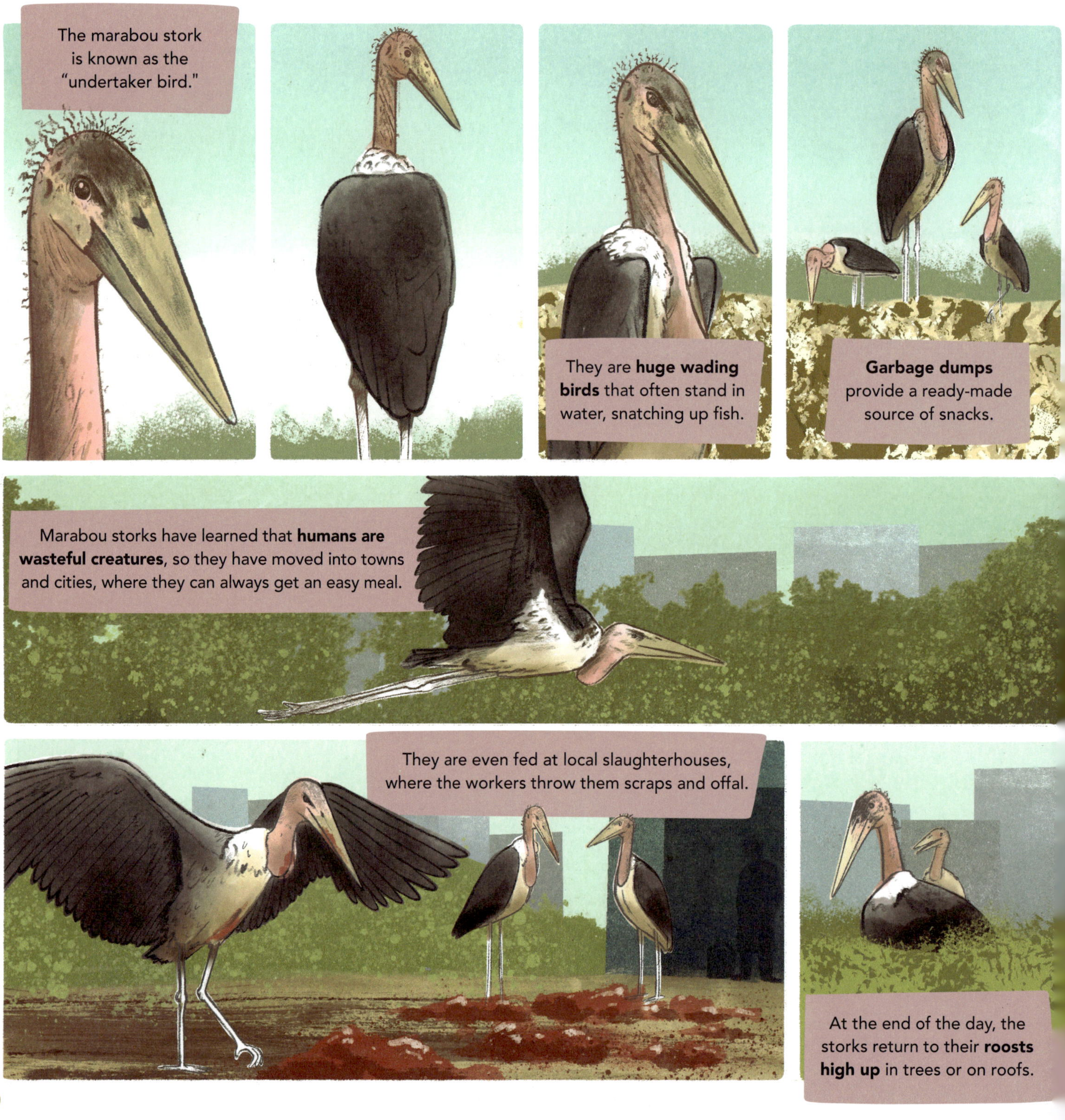
The marabou stork is known as the "undertaker bird."
They are **huge wading birds** that often stand in water, snatching up fish.
Garbage dumps provide a ready-made source of snacks.
Marabou storks have learned that **humans are wasteful creatures**, so they have moved into towns and cities, where they can always get an easy meal.
They are even fed at local slaughterhouses, where the workers throw them scraps and offal.
At the end of the day, the storks return to their **roosts high up** in trees or on roofs.

Marabou Stork Fact File

Latin name:	***Leptoptilos crumeniferus***
Origin:	**Africa, south of the Sahara desert**
Habitat:	**Grasslands and near water**
Size:	**Up to 5 ft. (1.5 m) tall**
Lifespan:	**Up to 25 years**
Diet:	**Carrion and human food waste. Also preys on fish, reptiles, and insects.**
Predators:	**None, although lions and leopards occasionally attack them.**
Curiosity:	**One of the world's largest birds, the marabou stork has a wingspan of almost 10 ft. (3 m).**

Like vultures, marabou storks have a bald head and neck. This makes it easier to keep themselves clean of blood and bacteria after feeding on a carcass.

Delicious dung beetles lurk inside lumps of smelly elephant dung. Marabous drop balls of dung into water to wash the poop away so they can gobble down the beetles.

This bird's saggy, baggy throat pouch is used at mating time. It can be inflated with air, like a balloon, and used to make loud croaking sounds.

Africa's grasslands are sweltering in the midday sun. Marabous cool down by releasing white liquid poop down their legs.

Spotlight on:

VULTURES

With their bald heads and hooked beaks, vultures do a very important job. When these scavengers clean up dead and rotting animals, they reduce the spread of diseases. There are 23 species of vulture, and sadly, half of them are at risk of extinction.

Griffon Vulture
When these bulky birds gather around the body of an animal, they squabble loudly, fighting to get close enough to dig in and tear at the meat.

Old World Vultures

Old World vultures live in Africa, Europe, and Asia. Like most birds, they use their superb eyesight to find food. They also follow predators, such as lions and wolves, and dive in for a meal once the hunt is over and the predators have left their kill.

Lappet-Faced Vulture
Not only does this fearsome vulture scavenge, but it is also powerful enough to hunt and kill its own prey.

Bearded Vulture
Bearded vultures mostly eat bones, often dropping them from a great height so they break open and the birds can get to the soft, juicy marrow inside.

Hooded Vulture
This small vulture is critically endangered, which means its numbers are falling fast and it is at great risk of going extinct.

Egyptian Vulture
Egyptian vultures use stones to smash open bird eggs, and they even drop tortoises onto rocks to crack their shells open. They also eat animal scat and rotting fruit.

New World Vultures

There are seven species of New World vultures, including two condors, and they all live in the Americas. Most of them have an excellent sense of smell and can sniff out a dead animal from afar, even in a dense jungle.

Turkey Vulture
This bird uses its sense of smell to find and feast on roadkill—animals that have been killed by cars and trucks.

Andean Condor
The Andean condor has the largest wingspan of any bird. Like most other vultures, it uses its large wings to soar high in the sky.

Black Vulture
Black vultures have long, slender beaks that they use to pick off every tiny bit of flesh from a carcass, leaving the bones clean.

Amazing Adaptations

The digestive system can break down deadly bacteria, making the bacteria harmless.

Heavy brows protect the eyes from the sun's glare.
A strong, hooked beak is perfect for ripping skin and flesh.
Fluffy feathers would get covered in blood, so a vulture has a bald head and neck.
Using its long neck, a vulture can get its head deep inside a carcass.
Long, broad wings allow vultures to save energy by soaring on warm air currents.
Acid in their scat, or poop, can kill bacteria.
Weak, almost flat feet for standing on a carcass.

Vultures at Risk

Vultures are true heroes of the cleanup crew. They help keep our world healthy and clean, but these bold, hardworking birds have been poisoned and hunted all over the world.

Since the 1990s, India's population of white-rumped vultures has crashed by 99 percent, owing to poisoning.

About 1,000 griffon vultures die every year in Spain after flying into wind turbines.

Deadly medicines
Diclofenac is a medicine given to cattle. It is toxic to vultures that feed on their carcasses.

Poisons and poaching
Poachers put poison on the animals they kill to stop vultures from giving away their position. Farmers also poison predators that attack their livestock. This then kills vultures that feed on them.

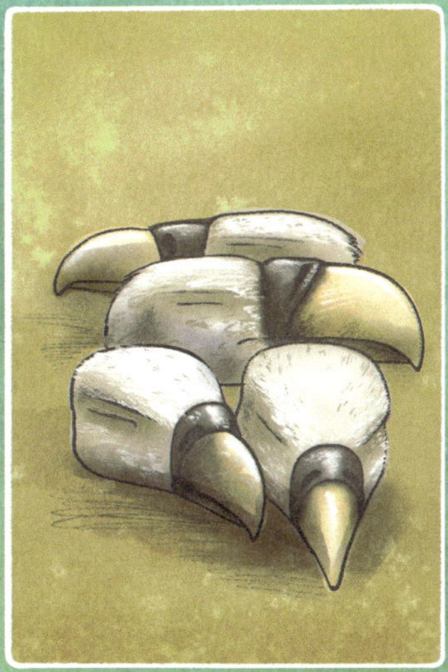

Hunting
In some cultures, people believe that vultures' body parts can be used to cure diseases and in magic spells.

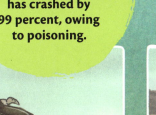

Accidents
Vultures die when they fly into power lines and wind turbines or get hit by cars and trains.

The Ocean Cleanup Crew

When a whale dies, its huge body becomes an incredible ecosystem. Scavengers visit to feast on the mammal's flesh, and an army of smaller creatures arrive to set up home on the carcass. Known as "whale fall," this ocean event brings life to the seabed and returns nutrients and energy to the ocean.

A whale has just died. The gases inside its body expand, and the **carcass floats up to the surface**, bloated and swollen.
Seabirds pick at it, and **sharks** gather to rip off chunks of flesh.
The whale carcass begins to sink.
Slowly it falls **deeper and deeper** into the cold, black water.
The carcass finally comes to rest on the seabed, and a **new set of scavengers** arrives.
Hagfish, sharks, and lobsters start to feed on the meat.

Sea cucumbers devour the **detritus** while other creatures, such as **brittle stars**, scrape away at the carcass, bit by bit.

Amphipods arrive to pick the bones clean. They attract **predators**, such as **octopuses**, which come to feed on the scavengers.

Zombie worms dig into the bones, using acid to dissolve holes in them. Thanks to bacteria that live in their bodies, the worms can extract nutrients from the bones.

Now it's time for **bacteria** and other **microbes** to complete the job of decomposing the carcass. **Sea snails and shellfish** feed on the bacteria.

It can take **50 to 100 years** for a whale carcass to completely decompose.

Christmas Tree Worm

Who knew that worms could be this colorful?

Christmas tree worms live on corals and shimmer in a variety of colors. The feathery, treelike body parts are feeding tentacles, called radioles. The rest of the worm's body is hidden from view in a tube tucked into the rocky coral.

Christmas Tree Worm Fact File

Latin name:	***Spirobranchus giganteus***
Origin:	**Tropical oceans and seas**
Habitat:	**Shallow reef waters**
Size:	**Up to 1½ in. (35 mm)**
Lifespan:	**10–50 years**
Diet:	**Fish, insects, worms, snails, and other axolotls**
Predators:	**Fish, sea urchins, crabs, and other crustaceans**
Curiosity:	**Can regrow its radioles.**

The worms come in shades of yellow, red, green, orange, and blue.

The radioles take oxygen from seawater. They also collect detritus and plankton, passing the food into the worm's mouth.

The worms have orange eyespots dotted along their radioles. These eyespots detect shadows passing overhead, which warns a worm that there is danger.

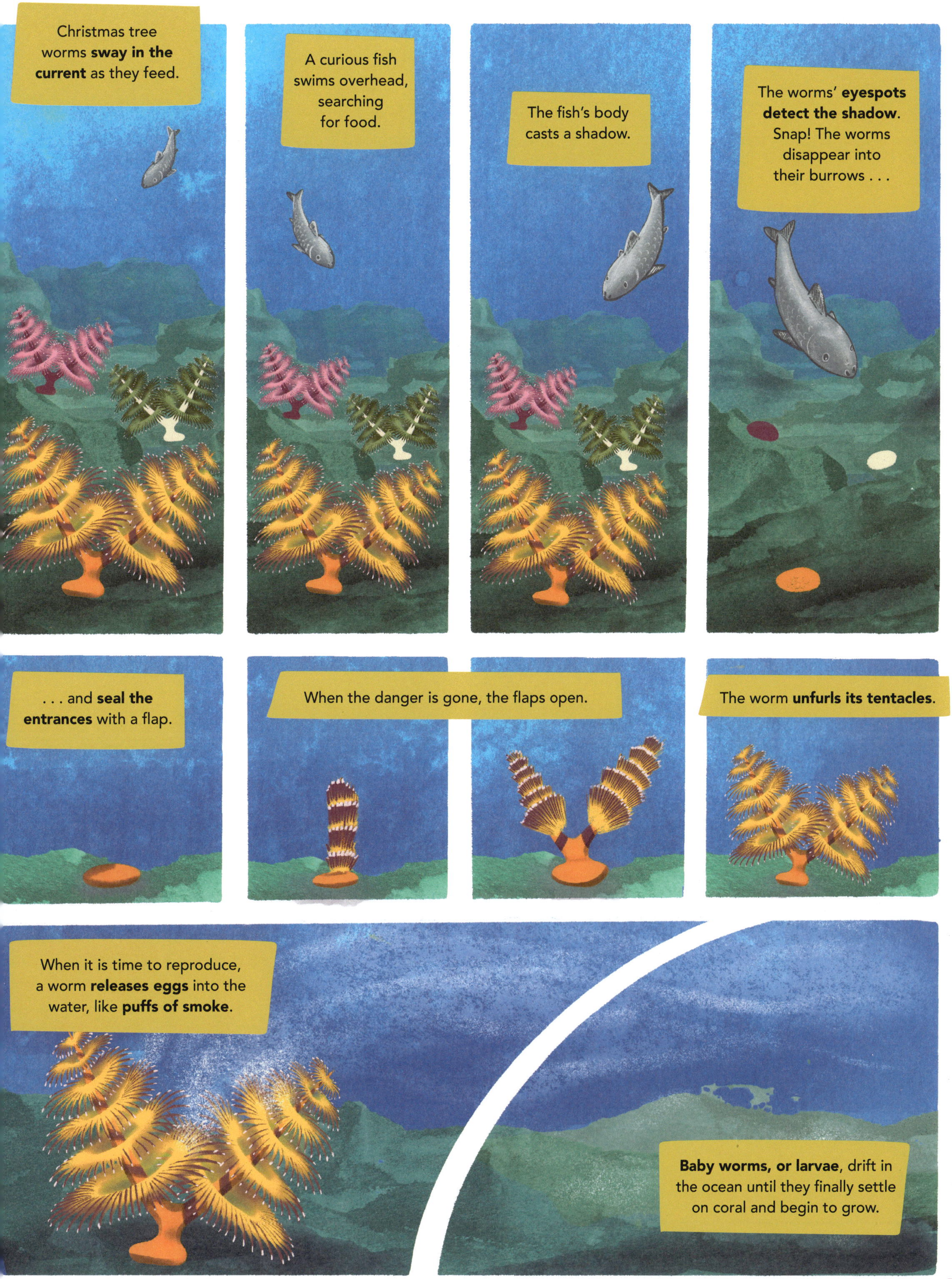
Christmas tree worms **sway in the current** as they feed.
A curious fish swims overhead, searching for food.
The fish's body casts a shadow.
The worms' **eyespots detect the shadow**. Snap! The worms disappear into their burrows . . .
. . . and **seal the entrances** with a flap.
When the danger is gone, the flaps open.
The worm **unfurls its tentacles**.
When it is time to reproduce, a worm **releases eggs** into the water, like **puffs of smoke**.
Baby worms, or larvae, drift in the ocean until they finally settle on coral and begin to grow.

Tiger Shark

The "trash can" with fins

Tiger sharks are fearsome predators, but they are most famous for their scavenging habits—these large fish are not picky eaters. They scavenge to save themselves the hassle of hunting, but not everything they eat is food. Tiger sharks have been known to swallow bottles, cans, old car tires, and even a sack of potatoes.

Tiger Shark Fact File

Latin name:	***Galeocerdo cuvier***
Origin:	**Oceans, estuaries, and harbors**
Habitat:	**Tropical and temperate waters, especially near the coast**
Size:	**Up to 18 ft. (5.5 m)**
Lifespan:	**More than 30 years**
Diet:	**Fish, turtles, sea snakes, marine mammals, birds, jellyfish, carrion, and garbage**
Predators:	**Humans**
Curiosity:	**A mother tiger shark can give birth to more than 80 pups at a time.**

This shark is named after the dark stripes on its back and sides. They fade as the shark gets older.
Tiger sharks travel great distances to reach the places where turtles and seabirds will be laying eggs on the beach.
This shark's teeth are serrated, like a saw. Once it has cau its prey, it shakes its h from side to side to t off large chunks of flesh.

Every year, thousands of green sea turtles gather on Raine Island, in the Great Barrier Reef, to lay their eggs in the soft sand.
Each female can lay up to 200 eggs—it's exhausting work.
Most of them clamber back to the sea and swim away . . .
. . . but the weaker ones die on the shore or in the shallows.
The tide washes a carcass out to sea, and a tiger shark lies in wait.
It ignores the healthy turtles that are swimming away. The shark has set its eyes on an easier target: dead turtles.
Using its immense jaws and impressive teeth, the shark quickly crunches through a turtle's tough shell.
With a full belly, the shark sets off on its journey to find more food.

Sea cucumbers feed on detritus and small particles of food that float past them. They catch their food using tentacles that grow around the mouth.

The sea cucumbers on one reef can sort and clean 50,000 tons of sediment in just one year.

There are at least 1,800 species of sea cucumbers. They are echinoderms, which means they are related to starfish and sea urchins.

Sea cucumbers don't have a brain or eyes, but theys, but sea cucumbers do have many tube feet that they use to crawl on the seabed.

Sea Cucumber

This squirty superstar eats dirty sand and cleans it

Sea cucumbers may look like sausages with tentacles, but they are one of the ocean's greatest treasures. They scoot around the seabed, sucking up dirty sand like a vacuum cleaner and pooping out clean sand. Disease-free and healthy, this sand can be used by animals that build coral reefs.

Sea Cucumber Fact File

Latin name:	***Bohadschia argus***
Origin:	**Oceans and seas worldwide**
Habitat:	**The seabed**
Size:	**Varies, but the average is 8 in. (20 cm)**
Lifespan:	**Up to 10 years**
Diet:	**Detritus and plankton**
Predators:	**Fish, crabs, turtles, and humans**
Curiosity:	**Blue sea cucumbers have five sharp teeth on their rear to stop parasite fish from setting up home inside their gut!**

Sneaky pearlfish swim into a sea cucumber's body through its bottom and set up home. Some pearlfish do no harm, but others start to eat the echinoderm from the inside out.

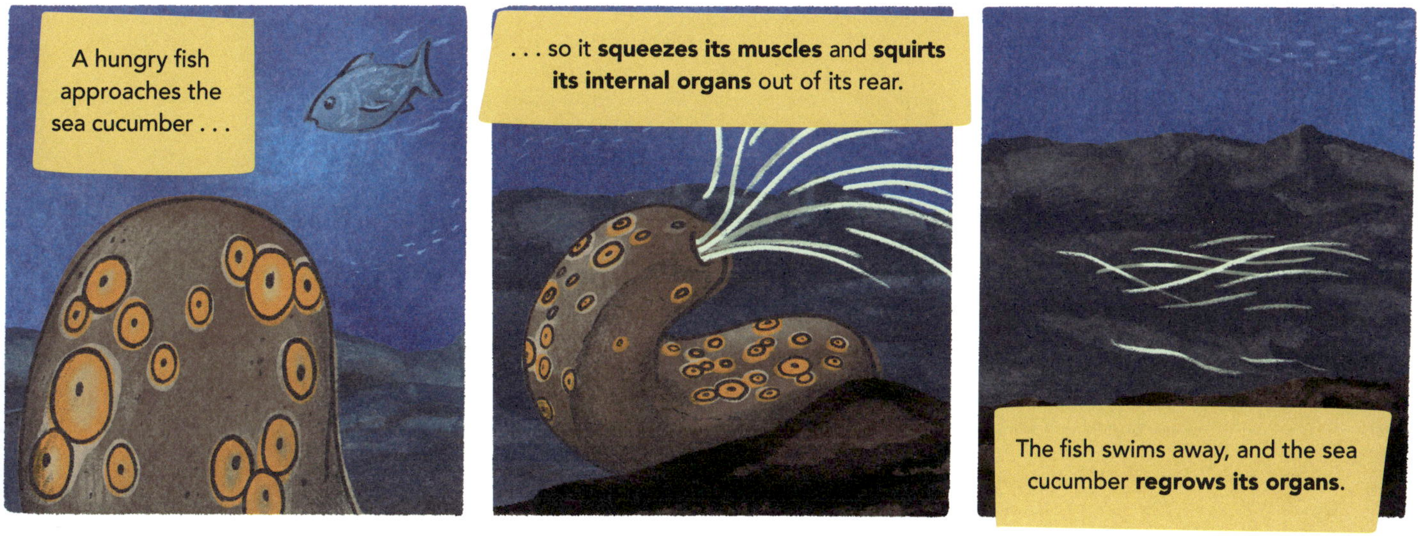
A hungry fish approaches the sea cucumber . . .
. . . so it **squeezes its muscles** and **squirts its internal organs** out of its rear.
The fish swims away, and the sea cucumber **regrows its organs**.

Spotlight on:

CRABS AND LOBSTERS

An army of armor-plated animals swims, creeps, and crawls through the world's oceans, cleaning up the seabed. Crabs and lobsters are types of crustaceans—animals with toughened skin. Many of them have a pair of large claws for hunting and scavenging.

Brown Crab

Brown crabs crush tough shells of mussels and sea urchins to get to the soft flesh inside, but they also scavenge carrion and detritus from the seabed.

Spiny Lobster

Spiny lobsters have very long antennae and lack a pair of large pincer claws. They usually hide in cracks and crevices during the day, coming out at night to hunt or scavenge.

Spiny lobsters are social animals and often live in groups of 12 or more. They march across the seabed in lines when migrating.

American Lobster

These large lobsters have four pairs of walking legs and a pair of legs with giant claws for tearing and crunching. They hunt other small animals and eat carrion.

Decorator Crab

These clever crabs don't just scavenge for food to eat, they collect all sorts of materials from the seabed and decorate themselves with it. This makes an excellent camouflage and allows them to hide from predators.

Hermit Crab

Hermit crabs are great at reducing and recycling waste! They not only nibble on detritus that litters the sea floor, but they also put old shells to good use, turning them into cozy homes.

Safely tucked inside a shell, a hermit crab is hidden from larger predators.
When a hermit crab outgrows its shell, it must find a new, larger shell to move into.
Moving to a new home is a dangerous time for hermit crabs, so they swap shells as fast as they can.

A hermit crab finds a **new shell**, which means its old shell will be available for a smaller crab.

More **hermit crabs line up**, each one ready to upgrade to the next size of shell.

Ready, set, go! The **big swap** begins, and everyone **scrambles out of their old shell**.

If all goes well, everyone gets a new shell and the hermit crabs **scuttle back to the sea**.

The Woodland Cleanup Crew

More than 2,000 types of animals, plants, and fungi can make their home in a healthy tree. When a tree dies, its story doesn't come to an end—it will continue to be a precious habitat for decades to come.

Tree holes in dying or dead trees make for the perfect home for many birds, including woodpeckers, hornbills, and owls.

It may take years for a tree to die. After it has died, it may fall over or stay standing for years to come. It is called **"dead wood."**

Beetles bore into the bark and the wood beneath.

The holes in the tree allow water, fungi, and bacteria to get into the tree.

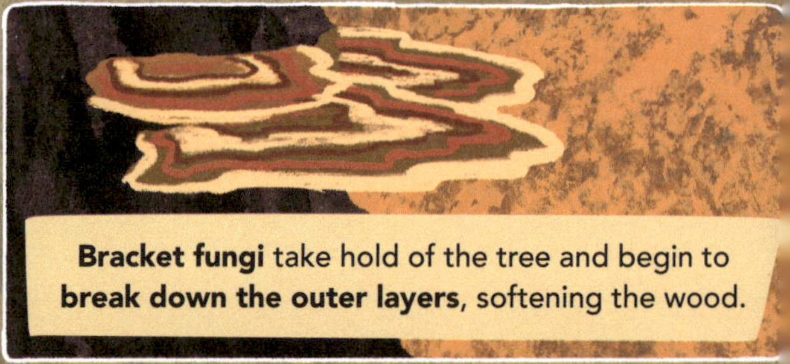

Bracket fungi take hold of the tree and begin to **break down the outer layers**, softening the wood.

This makes it easier for many organisms, including other fungi and more beetles, to feast on the tree.

It can take 100 years for a tree to decompose.

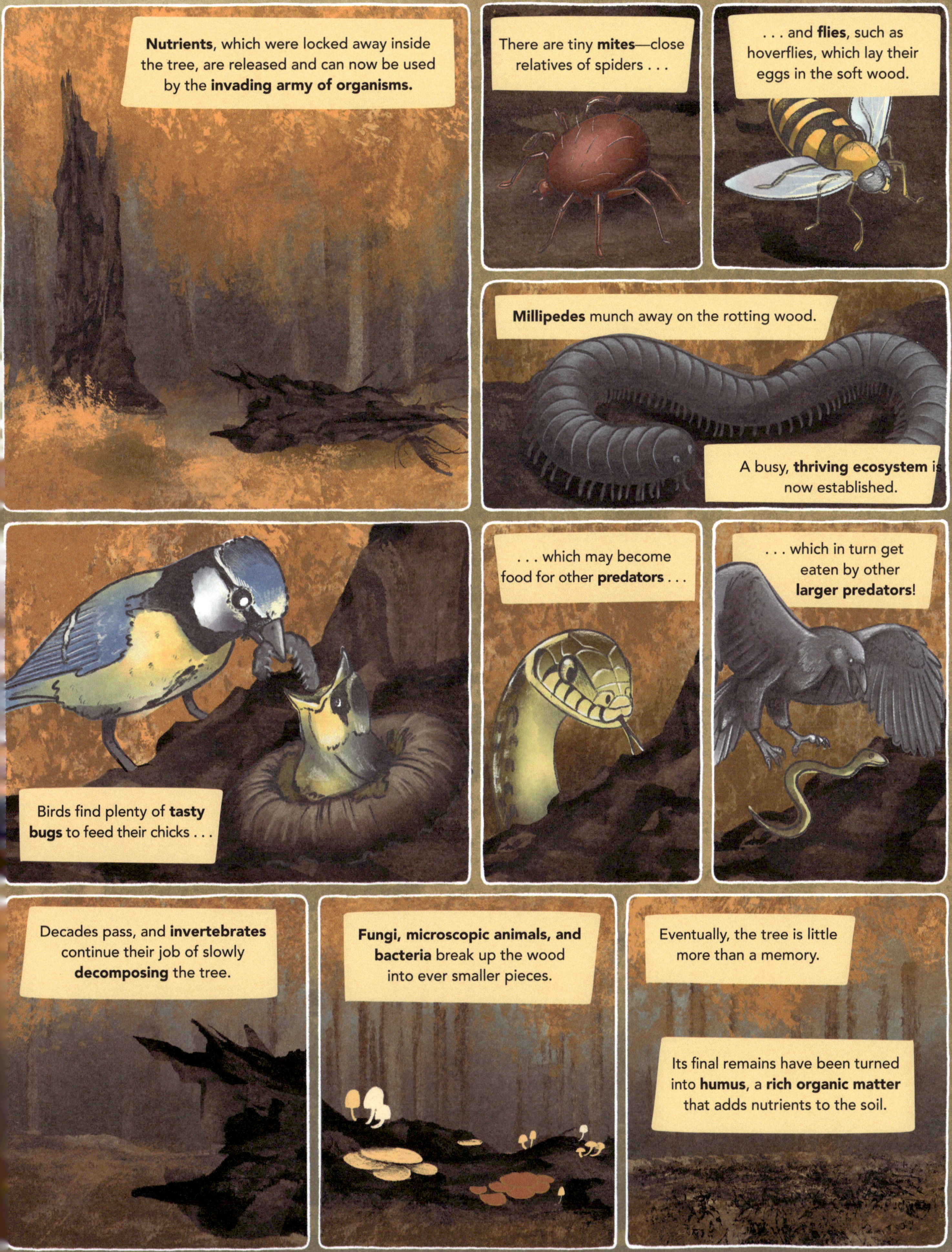
Nutrients, which were locked away inside the tree, are released and can now be used by the **invading army of organisms.**
There are tiny **mites**—close relatives of spiders . . .
. . . and **flies**, such as hoverflies, which lay their eggs in the soft wood.
Millipedes munch away on the rotting wood.
A busy, **thriving ecosystem** is now established.
Birds find plenty of **tasty bugs** to feed their chicks . . .
. . . which may become food for other **predators** . . .
. . . which in turn get eaten by other **larger predators**!
Decades pass, and **invertebrates** continue their job of slowly **decomposing** the tree.
Fungi, microscopic animals, and bacteria break up the wood into ever smaller pieces.
Eventually, the tree is little more than a memory.
Its final remains have been turned into **humus**, a **rich organic matter** that adds nutrients to the soil.

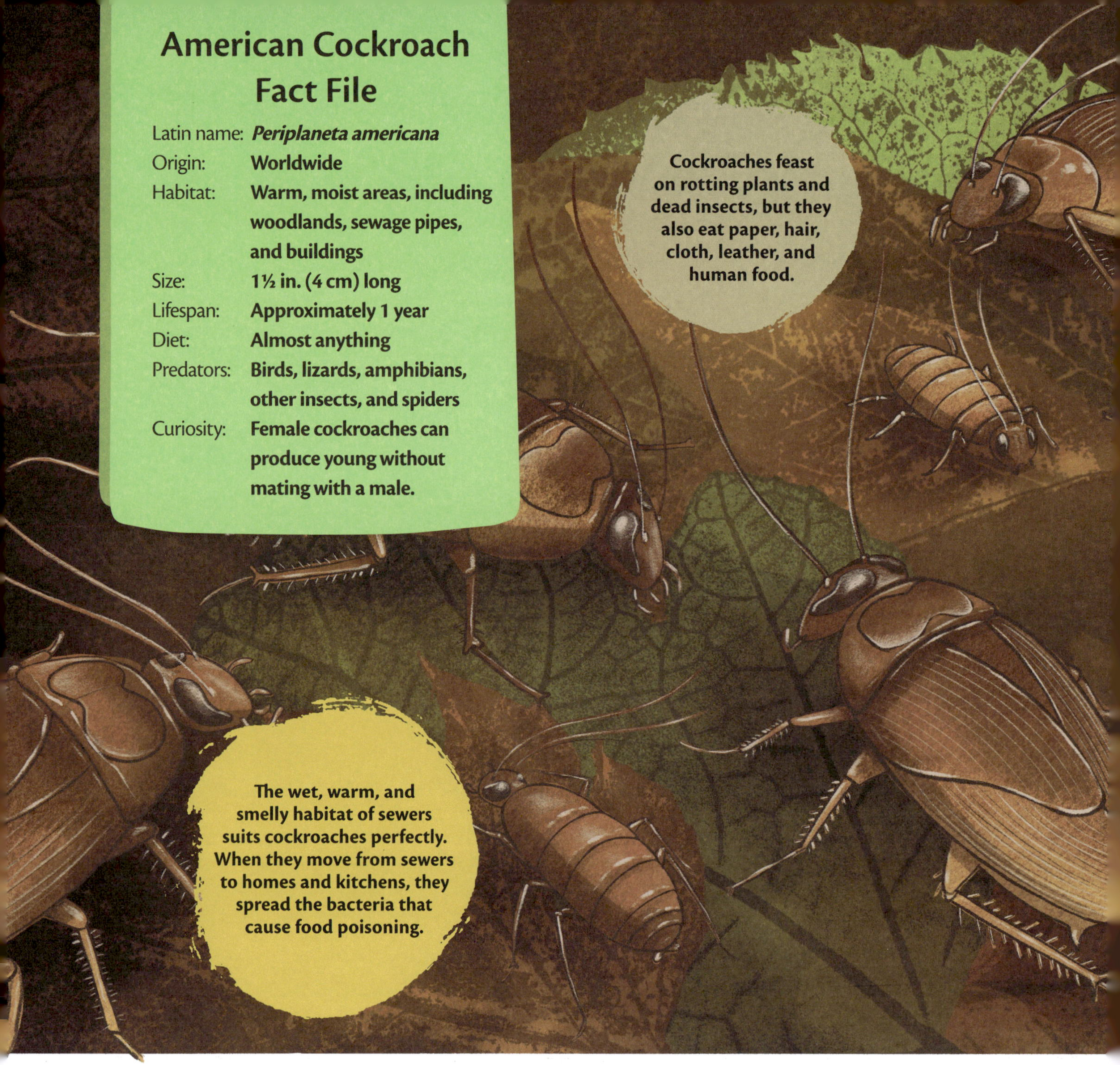

American Cockroach Fact File

Latin name:	***Periplaneta americana***
Origin:	**Worldwide**
Habitat:	**Warm, moist areas, including woodlands, sewage pipes, and buildings**
Size:	**1½ in. (4 cm) long**
Lifespan:	**Approximately 1 year**
Diet:	**Almost anything**
Predators:	**Birds, lizards, amphibians, other insects, and spiders**
Curiosity:	**Female cockroaches can produce young without mating with a male.**

Cockroaches feast on rotting plants and dead insects, but they also eat paper, hair, cloth, leather, and human food.

The wet, warm, and smelly habitat of sewers suits cockroaches perfectly. When they move from sewers to homes and kitchens, they spread the bacteria that cause food poisoning.

American Cockroach

These speedy insects are among the world's most successful animals

There are many reasons to be grateful to the world's cleanup crew, but cockroaches are far down most people's list of favorite scavengers and recyclers. Although they eat almost anything—including each other—in the natural world, they are hardworking decomposers. In human habitats, however, their scavenging habits can cause big problems, leading them to spread diseases.

Cockroaches run so fast they disappear before your eyes and are almost impossible to catch.

A **hungry bird** spies a tasty snack.
Crunch!
The **body of the cockroach** drops to the ground . . .
. . . and **stays alive for a week** or more. What a **survivor**!

Sexton Beetle

Nature's gravediggers

These busy bugs take great care of dead animals. They bury them, keep them clean, and even protect them from other members of the cleanup crew.

Sexton Beetle Fact File

Latin name:	***Genus Nicrophorus***
Origin:	**Europe, Asia, the Americas and northern Africa**
Habitat:	**Anywhere they can find carrion**
Size:	**Up to 1½ in. (40 mm)**
Lifespan:	**12 months**
Diet:	**Decaying plants and carrion**
Predators:	**Birds, reptiles, amphibians, small mammals and other invertebrates**
Curiosity:	**Can detect carrion from up to 1.9 miles (3 km) away.**

Unlike most insects, both sexton beetle parents take care of their young.

Sexton beetles are called the undertakers of the animal world. They tidy away dead bodies, making the world a cleaner place.

These beetles bury carcasses to stop other members of the cleanup crew from eating them, and to protect their own maggots from predators.

If sexton beetles have too many young for the carcass they have stored, they kill some of their maggots.

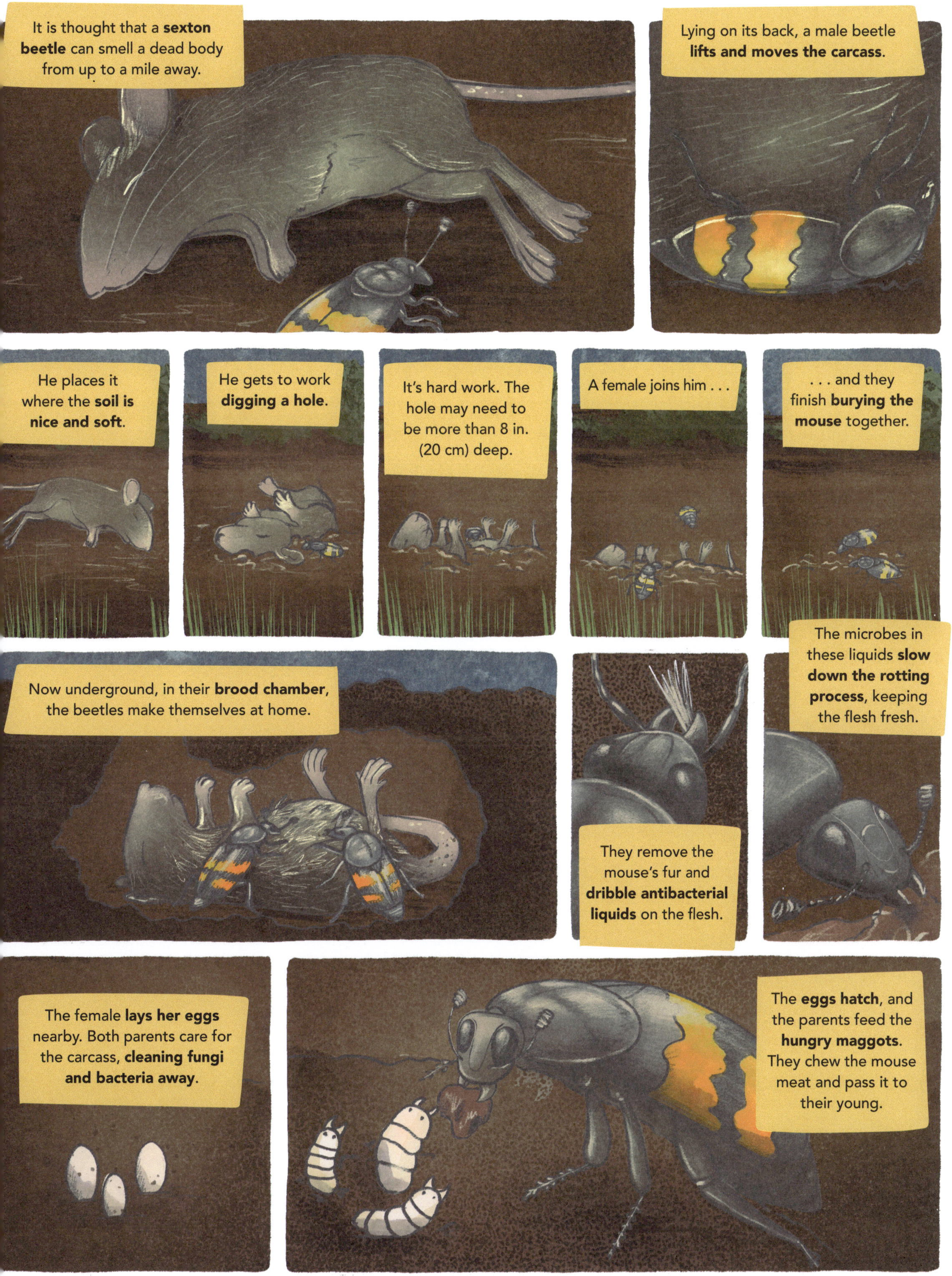
It is thought that a **sexton beetle** can smell a dead body from up to a mile away.
Lying on its back, a male beetle **lifts and moves the carcass**.
He places it where the **soil is nice and soft**.
He gets to work **digging a hole**.
It's hard work. The hole may need to be more than 8 in. (20 cm) deep.
A female joins him . . .
. . . and they finish **burying the mouse** together.
Now underground, in their **brood chamber**, the beetles make themselves at home.
They remove the mouse's fur and **dribble antibacterial liquids** on the flesh.
The microbes in these liquids **slow down the rotting process**, keeping the flesh fresh.
The female **lays her eggs** nearby. Both parents care for the carcass, **cleaning fungi and bacteria away**.
The **eggs hatch**, and the parents feed the **hungry maggots**. They chew the mouse meat and pass it to their young.

Spotlight on:

FUNGI

Most fungi are so small you need a microscope to look at them, but this varied group of living things also includes the largest organisms yet discovered. Fungi live everywhere, from the surface of your skin to the bottom of the sea, and most of them feed on dead matter.

Unlike plants, fungi cannot make their own food. They are more closely related to animals.

Mushrooms and Toadstools

Fruiting body
Mushrooms and toadstools are the fruiting body of a fungus. They make and release spores.
Gills
This is the part of the fruiting body where spores are made and released.
Mycelium
This is the main part of the fungus. It is a network of many hyphae.
Hyphae
These are slender white threads that grow into the fungus's food and make up the mycelium.

Mushroom spores are like a plant's seeds. They grow into new fungi.

Hyphae grow into the fungus's food and produce chemicals, called enzymes, that dissolve the food. The nutrients are then absorbed into the mycelium.

Mold

Fungi that grow on food are known as mold. Bread mold produces lots of little gray-black fruiting bodies that make the bread look furry, or "moldy."

Rot and Decay

Although some fungi thrive on living things, most fungi feed on dead organisms, recycling their nutrients back into the ecosystem. As they do this, the dead materials rot and decay. Fungi often work together with other members of the cleanup crew such as scavengers, detritivores, and bacteria.

An American honey fungus grows underground and in tree roots. It can grow to 2.4 miles (3.8 km) wide, making it the largest living thing on Earth.

Earpick Fungus
This fungus grows on pinecones and feeds on them.

Oak Leaf Pinwheel
This small fungus grows on dead oak leaves.

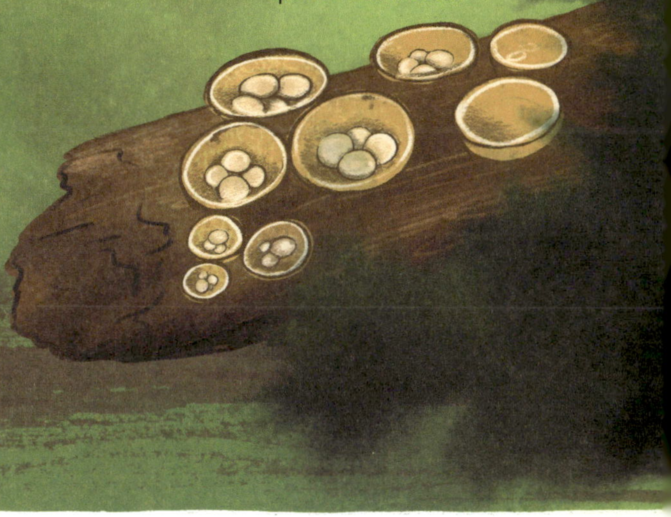

Bird's Nest Fungus
This woodland fungus looks like a tiny nest with eggs in it! It releases its spores when it rains.

3racket Fungi

racket fungi grow on both dead nd living trees. The fruiting odies are called brackets ue to its shape. They sually appear on a ee's trunk or main ranches. These ıngi can weaken or ven kill a healthy tree.

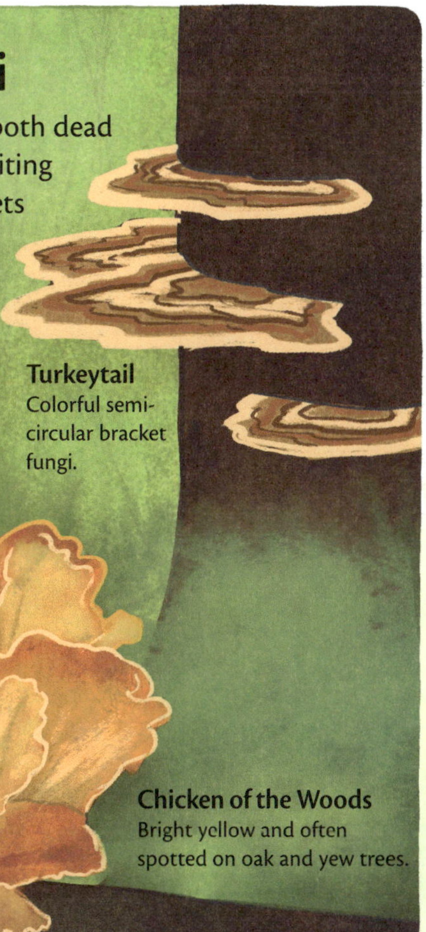

Turkeytail
Colorful semi-circular bracket fungi.

Chicken of the Woods
Bright yellow and often spotted on oak and yew trees.

Hat Thrower
Tosses its "hat" off to release its spores.

Humpback Inkcap
Grows on rotting wood and dung.

Snowy Inkcap
Often grows on old cow or horse dung.

Dung Lovers

Some fungi feed on animal dung, which helps keep our world clean. They are called coprophilous fungi, which means dung lovers!

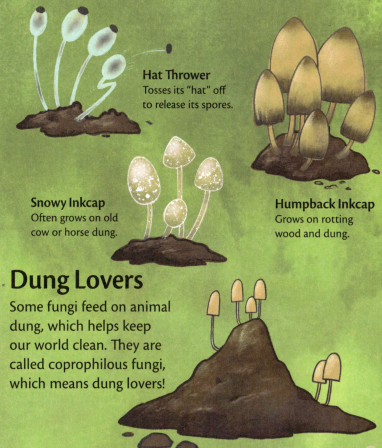

The Poop Cleanup Crew

Poop, poo, excrement, dung, feces—the smelly brown stuff has many names, and billions of tons of it are produced by animals everywhere. Meet the helpful dung beetles: nature's top pooper scoopers!

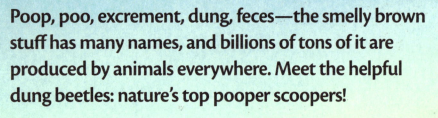

An elephant can produce ten times its own weight in poop every year.

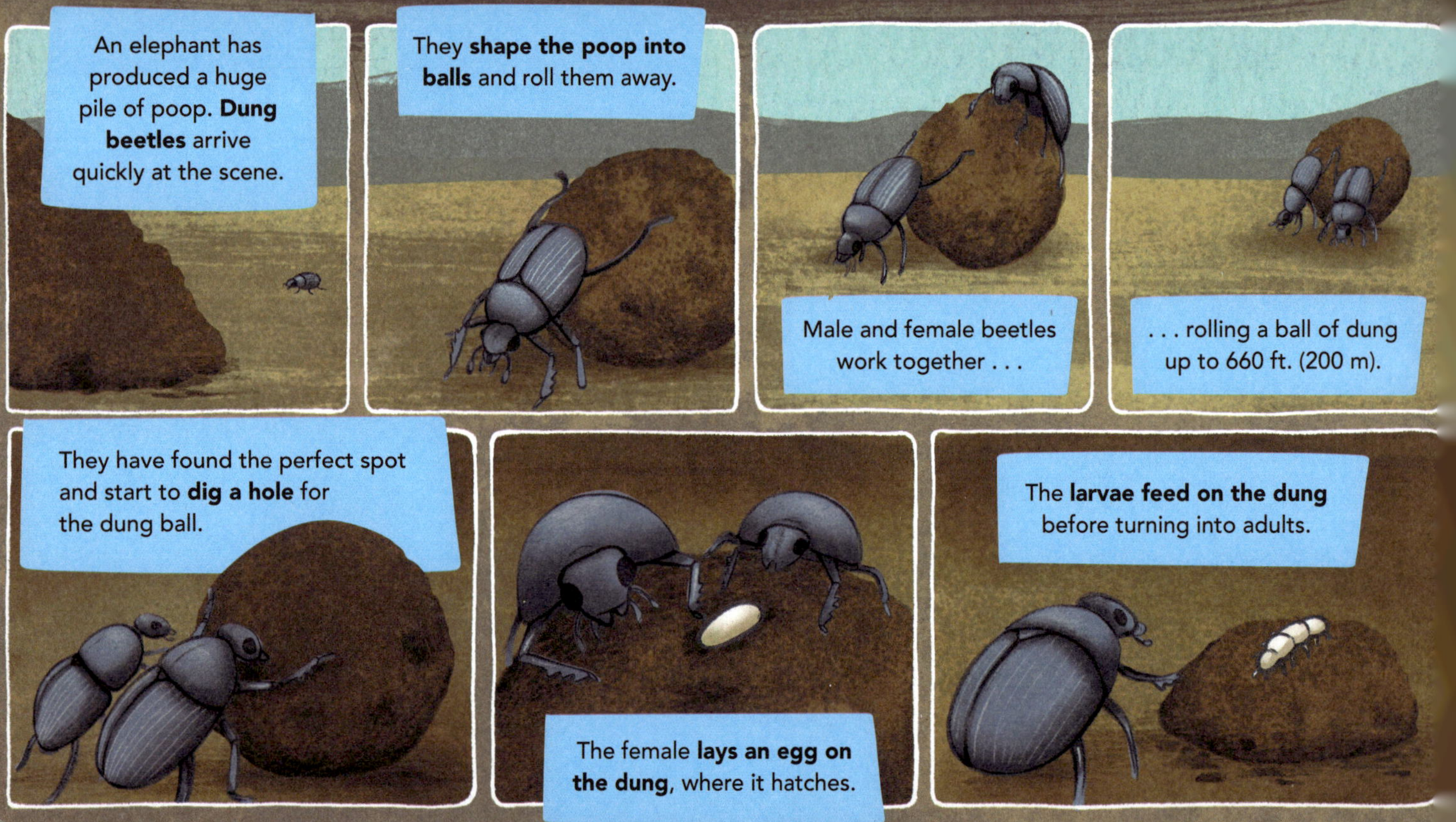
An elephant has produced a huge pile of poop. **Dung beetles** arrive quickly at the scene.
They **shape the poop into balls** and roll them away.
Male and female beetles work together . . .
. . . rolling a ball of dung up to 660 ft. (200 m).
They have found the perfect spot and start to **dig a hole** for the dung ball.
The female **lays an egg on the dung**, where it hatches.
The **larvae feed on the dung** before turning into adults.

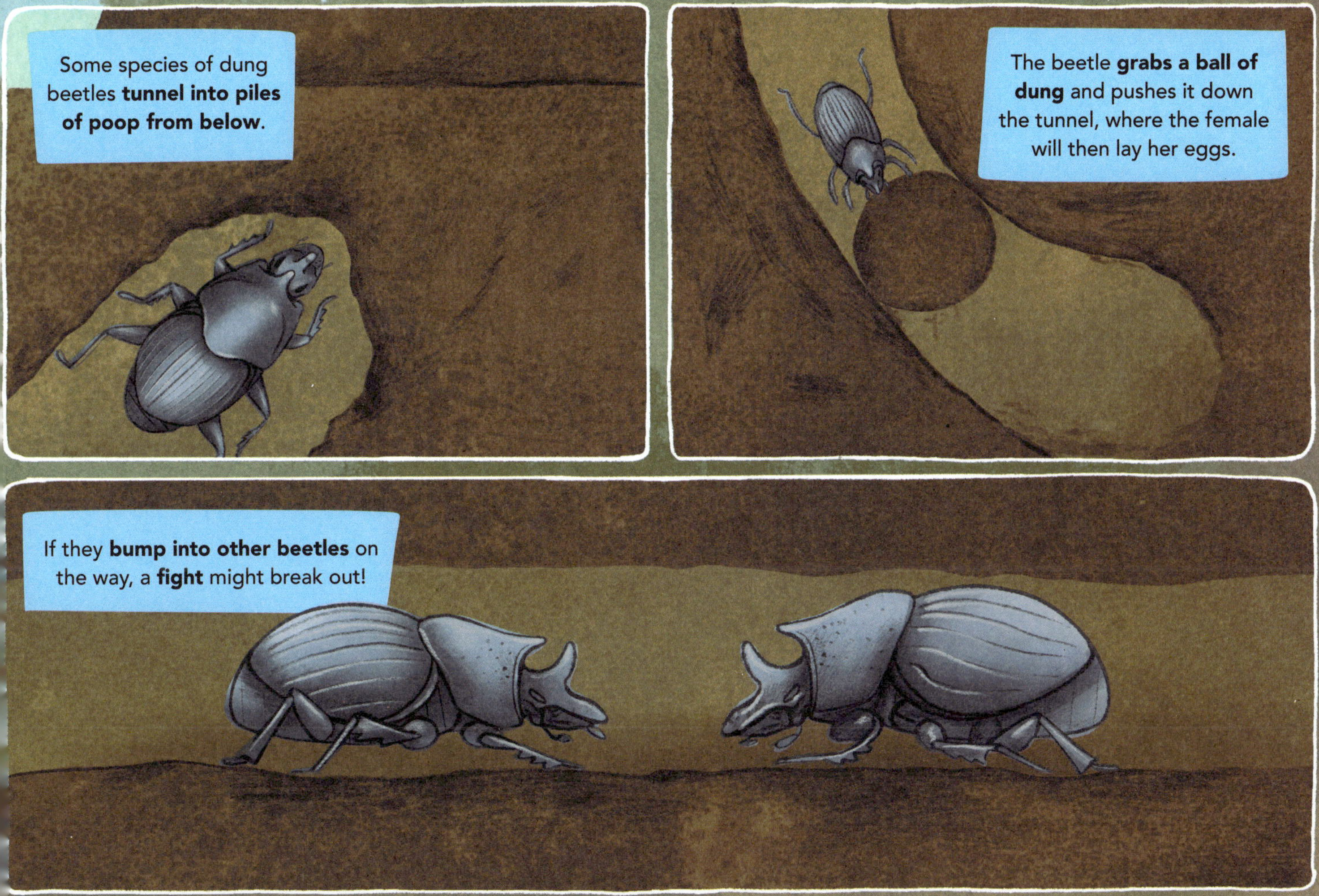

Some species of dung beetles **tunnel into piles of poop from below**.
The beetle **grabs a ball of dung** and pushes it down the tunnel, where the female will then lay her eggs.
If they **bump into other beetles** on the way, a **fight** might break out!

More Poop Crew Members

It is not just dung beetles that make a meal out of feces. Creatures that eat poop are called coprophages.

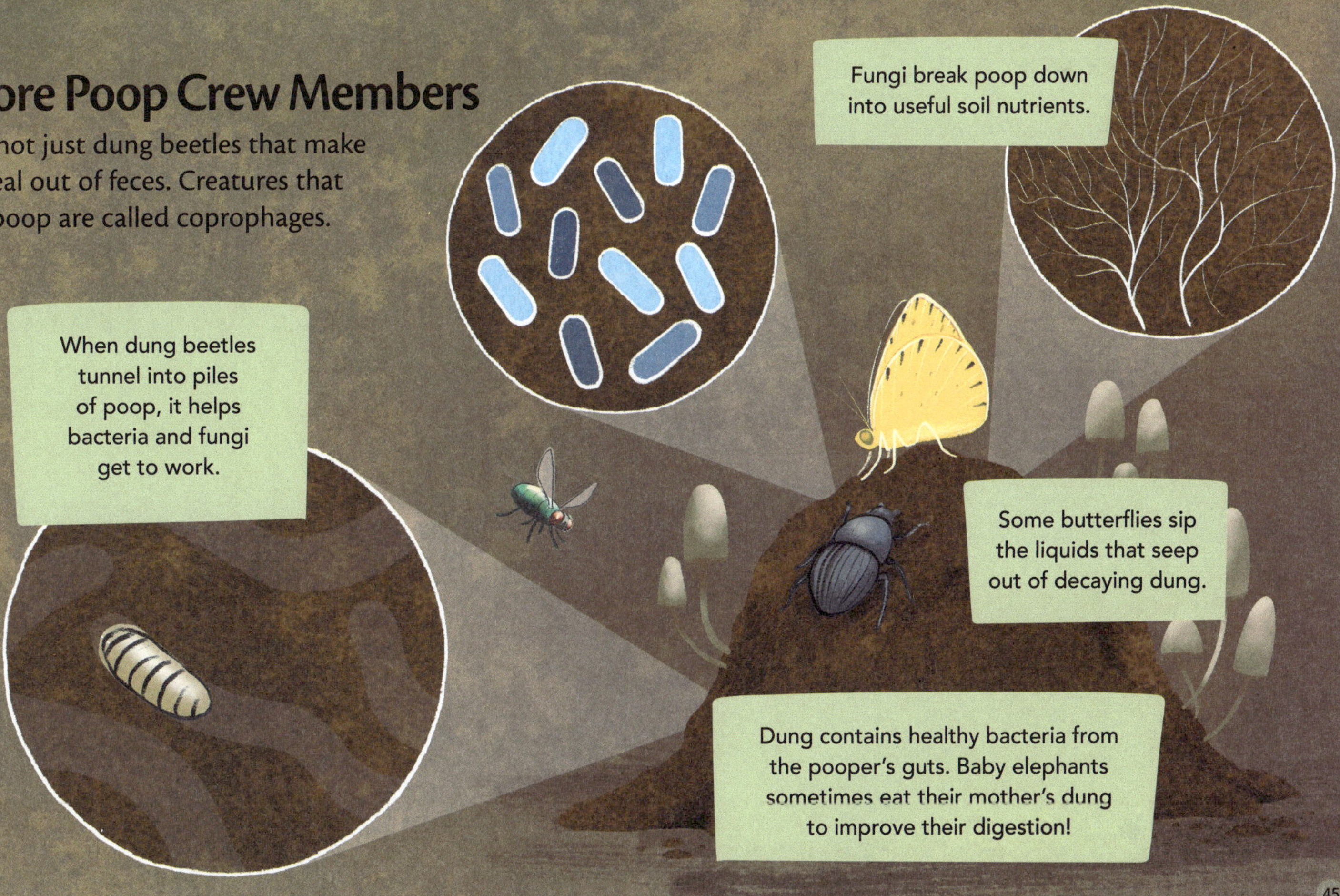

Fungi break poop down into useful soil nutrients.
When dung beetles tunnel into piles of poop, it helps bacteria and fungi get to work.
Some butterflies sip the liquids that seep out of decaying dung.
Dung contains healthy bacteria from the pooper's guts. Baby elephants sometimes eat their mother's dung to improve their digestion!

Earthworm

Wiggly wriggler and super soil muncher

An earthworm has no legs, no ears, and no eyes, and yet it is one of the world's most important creatures. Earthworms devour soil and small pieces of dead plants to extract nutrients. Then they produce perfect piles of poop, called worm casts, which are top-quality compost.

Earthworm Fact File

Latin name:	***Class Oligochaeta***
Origin:	**Worldwide**
Habitat:	**Leaf litter, mud, and soil**
Size:	**Usually 1–16 in. (2–40 cm) long**
Lifespan:	**Up to 8 years**
Diet:	**Detritus and soil**
Predators:	**Many, including birds, reptiles, amphibians, and other invertebrates**
Curiosity:	**Covered in slime, called mucus, which helps them slither through soil.**

As they burrow, worms bring air into the soil, keeping it healthy and allowing extra water to drain away, which helps prevent flooding.

An earthworm can die in just a few minutes if it is exposed to sunlight. They need damp, dark places!

An earthworm uses its soft, moist skin to breathe, see, smell, touch, and taste.

Scientists have found and named about 3,900 species of earthworms in the world. Some species of giant earthworms grow several yards long!

A worm's body is covered in tiny bristles, called setae, which it uses to wriggle through the soil.

Bluebottle

Shiny flies with munching maggots

The buzzing sound of a bluebottle is common on hot days, when these flies are on the prowl, searching for some rotting meat where they can lay their eggs.

Bluebottle Fact File

Latin names:	***Calliphora vomitoria* and *Calliphora vicina***
Origin:	**Worldwide**
Habitat:	**Anywhere they can feed**
Size:	**½ in. (10–14 mm)**
Lifespan:	**Up to 2 months**
Diet:	**Nectar and carrion**
Predators:	**Birds, reptiles, amphibians, and other invertebrates**
Curiosity:	**Some types of blowflies burrow into human skin and spread diseases.**

Bluebottles create their buzzing sound by beating their wings more than 100 times a second!

Bluebottles and greenbottles belong to a large group of insects called blowflies. They lay their eggs in decaying animal matter, including dung.

When bacteria rot meat, they produce heat. This heat warms the maggots up, helping them eat more and grow faster.

The **flies** smell a dead mouse . . .
. . . and **lay their eggs** on it.
The eggs **hatch**, and tiny **larvae emerge**. They are called **maggots**.
The maggots **eat the carrion**.
After just a few days, the maggots are **fully grown**.
They **crawl away** from the carcass.
The maggot is preparing for a **big change** . . .
. . . as it **buries itself** into the ground.
It grows a **tough skin** around itself. It is now called a **pupa**.
Inside, the maggot is turning into an **adult fly**.
After two weeks, the **fly emerges** from its hiding place.
It **spreads its wings** so they can dry.
The bluebottle flies off . . .
. . . only to be **snapped up** by a **hungry toad**!

Spotlight on:

BACTERIA

Microbes, or microorganisms, are any living things that are microscopic in size. Bacteria are a type of microbe and are among the world's most marvelous micro recyclers.

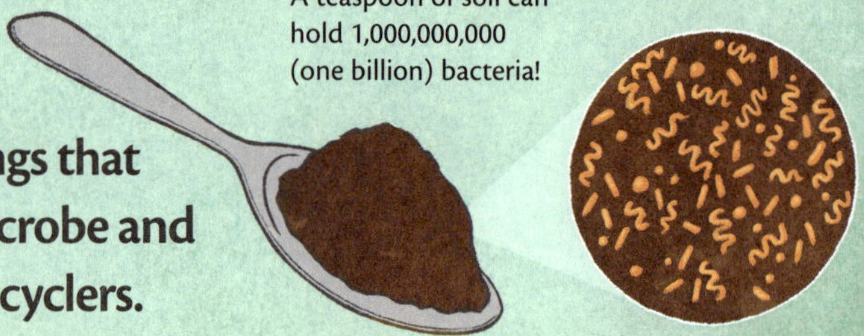

How small?
A teaspoon of soil can hold 1,000,000,000 (one billion) bacteria!

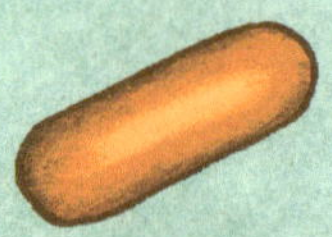

Bacteria
These are the smallest living things on Earth (except for viruses) and the oldest. They are found in every habitat, and they cause some diseases.

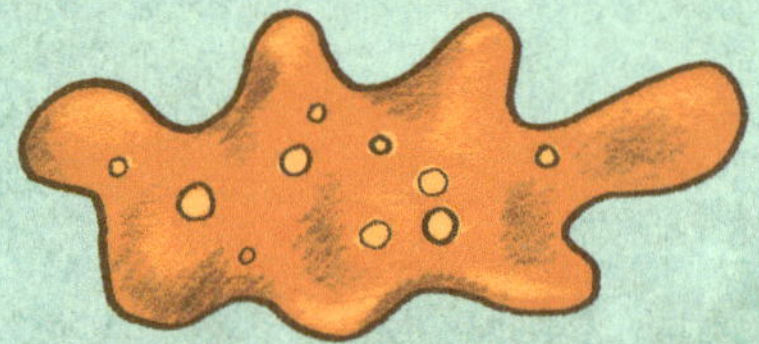

Protists
This group includes microscopic animals and plants. They are mostly made of just one cell and either eat food or make their own food.

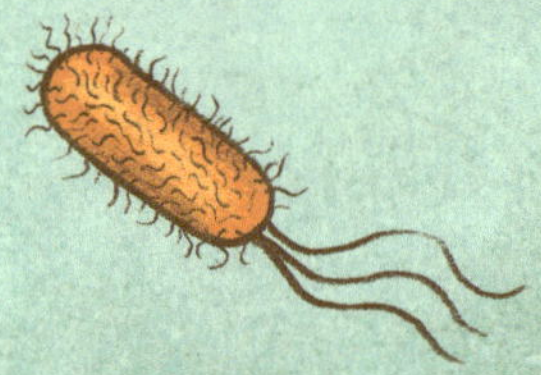

Archaea
These microorganisms look like bacteria. They live in soil, in oceans, and inside animals but don't cause diseases.

Bacteria have three basic shapes:

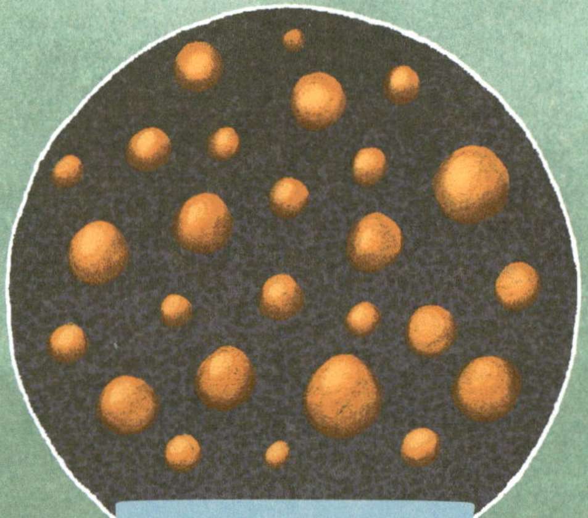

Spheres (ball-shaped)

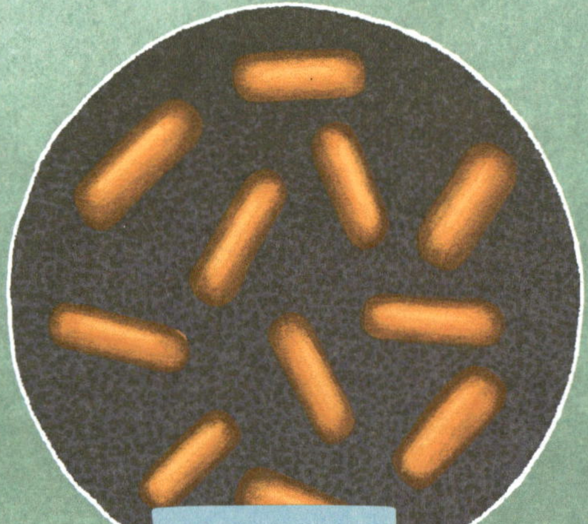

Rod-shaped

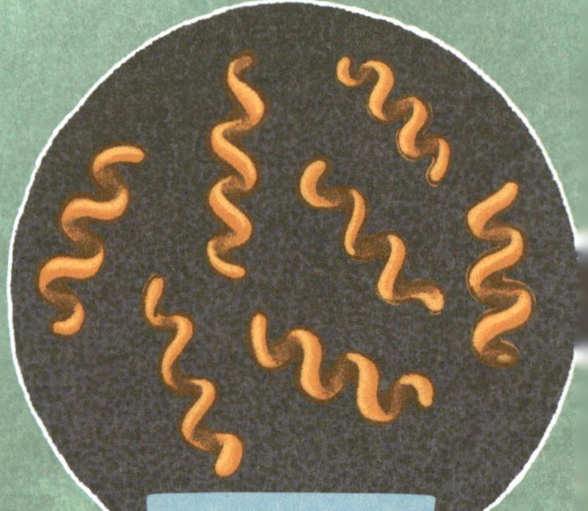

Spirals or helices

How do bacteria grow?

Bacteria grow by splitting themselves in half. In ideal conditions, they can do this every 20 minutes.

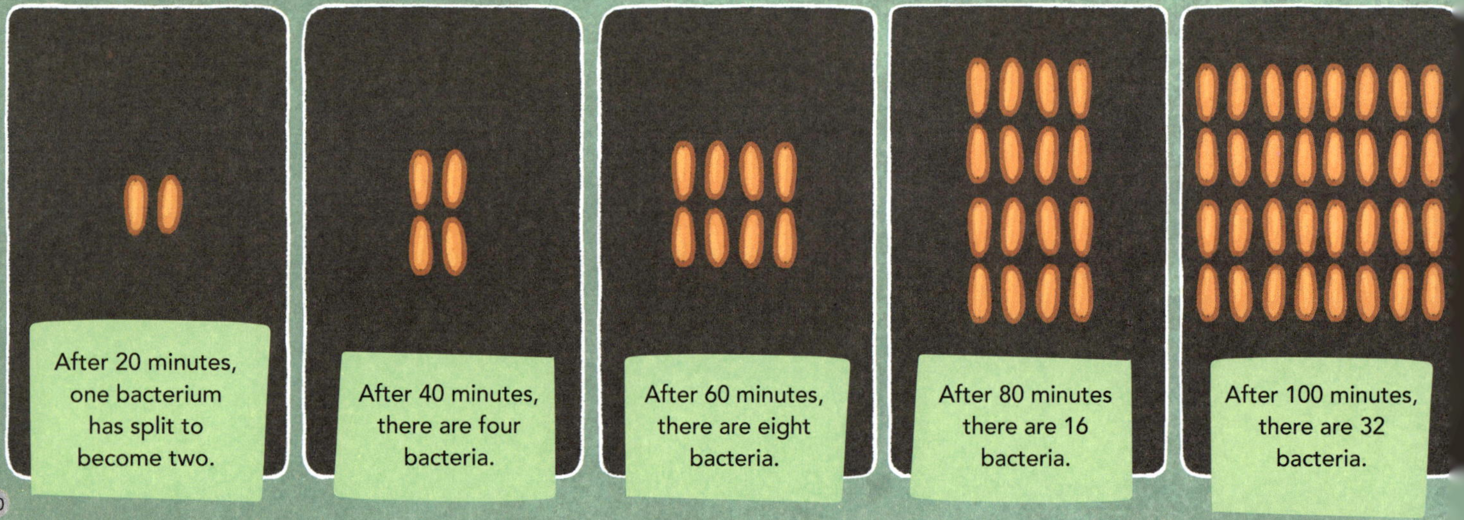

After 20 minutes, one bacterium has split to become two.

After 40 minutes, there are four bacteria.

After 60 minutes, there are eight bacteria.

After 80 minutes there are 16 bacteria.

After 100 minutes, there are 32 bacteria.

Pollution Problems

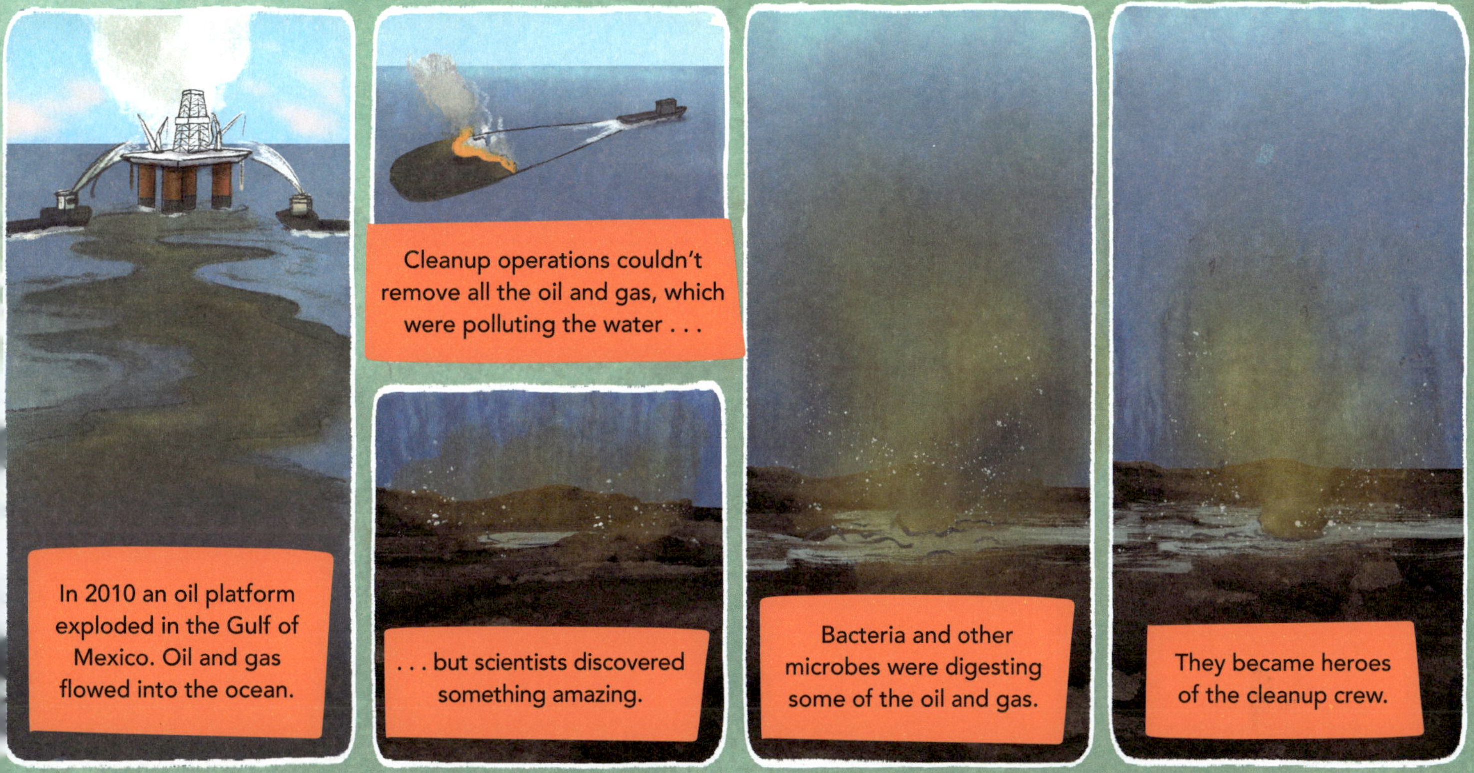
In 2010 an oil platform exploded in the Gulf of Mexico. Oil and gas flowed into the ocean.
Cleanup operations couldn't remove all the oil and gas, which were polluting the water . . .
. . . but scientists discovered something amazing.
Bacteria and other microbes were digesting some of the oil and gas.
They became heroes of the cleanup crew.

Humans fail to recycle most of the plastic we use. Thankfully, plastic-eating bacteria may one day be able to help us tackle this pollution problem. They break big pieces of plastic into smaller pieces, which they eat.

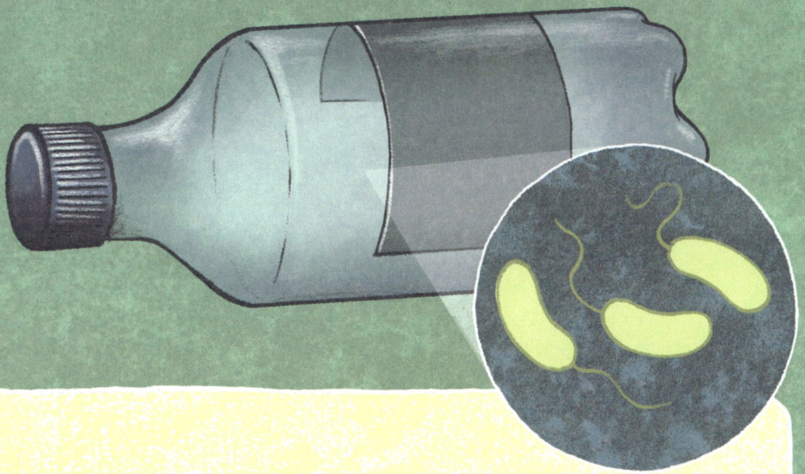

Bacteria and Food

When bacteria start to eat our food, they make it rot. They do this best in warm, damp environments.

Keeping food in the refrigerator slows down bacteria, helping food stay fresh and last longer.

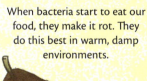

Pasteurization is a method of heating food to kill bacteria. Canning food (sealing and heating it in an airtight container) kills bacteria and stops more bacteria from reaching the food inside.

What Happens in a Compost Heap?

Magic happens inside the dark, warm, and wonderful environment of a compost heap. This is where a cleanup crew turns old, rotting matter into an earthy mix of nutrients, fiber, and organisms that feeds the soil and everything living in it.

Compost recipe

- **50% green stuff:** for example, plant cuttings, fruit and vegetable scraps
- **50% brown stuff:** for example, dry leaves, twigs, cardboard, wood chips, shredded paper
- **Air and water**

Mixing up the compost from time to time will help speed up the process.

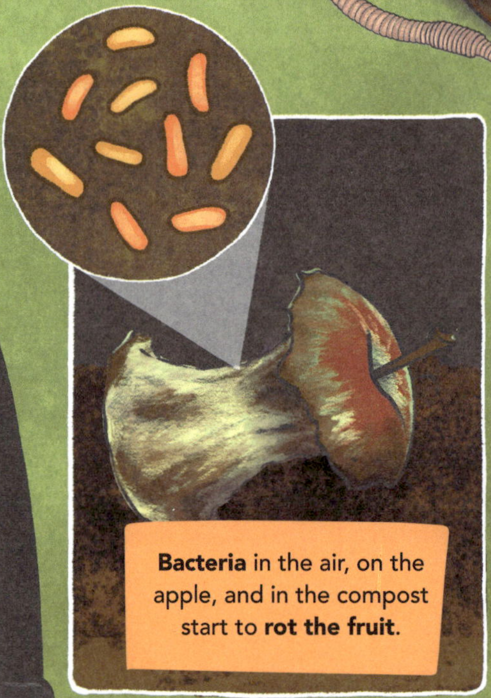
Bacteria in the air, on the apple, and in the compost start to **rot the fruit.**

Fungi grow hyphae into the apple, digesting it, and **invertebrates** also dig in.

Worms, pill bugs, beetles, millipedes, and **ants** get munching.

As more **waste is added** to the heap, the apple remains sink lower and continue to **decompose**.

Bacteria in the heap **create heat**. A warm habitat suits the cleanup crew, and they **work faster**.

Compost heroes

Inside the heap, all kinds of compost heroes are busy. Many-legged creatures scuttle between the layers, worms wriggle through tunnels, and small slugs slither around, chomping on the waste.

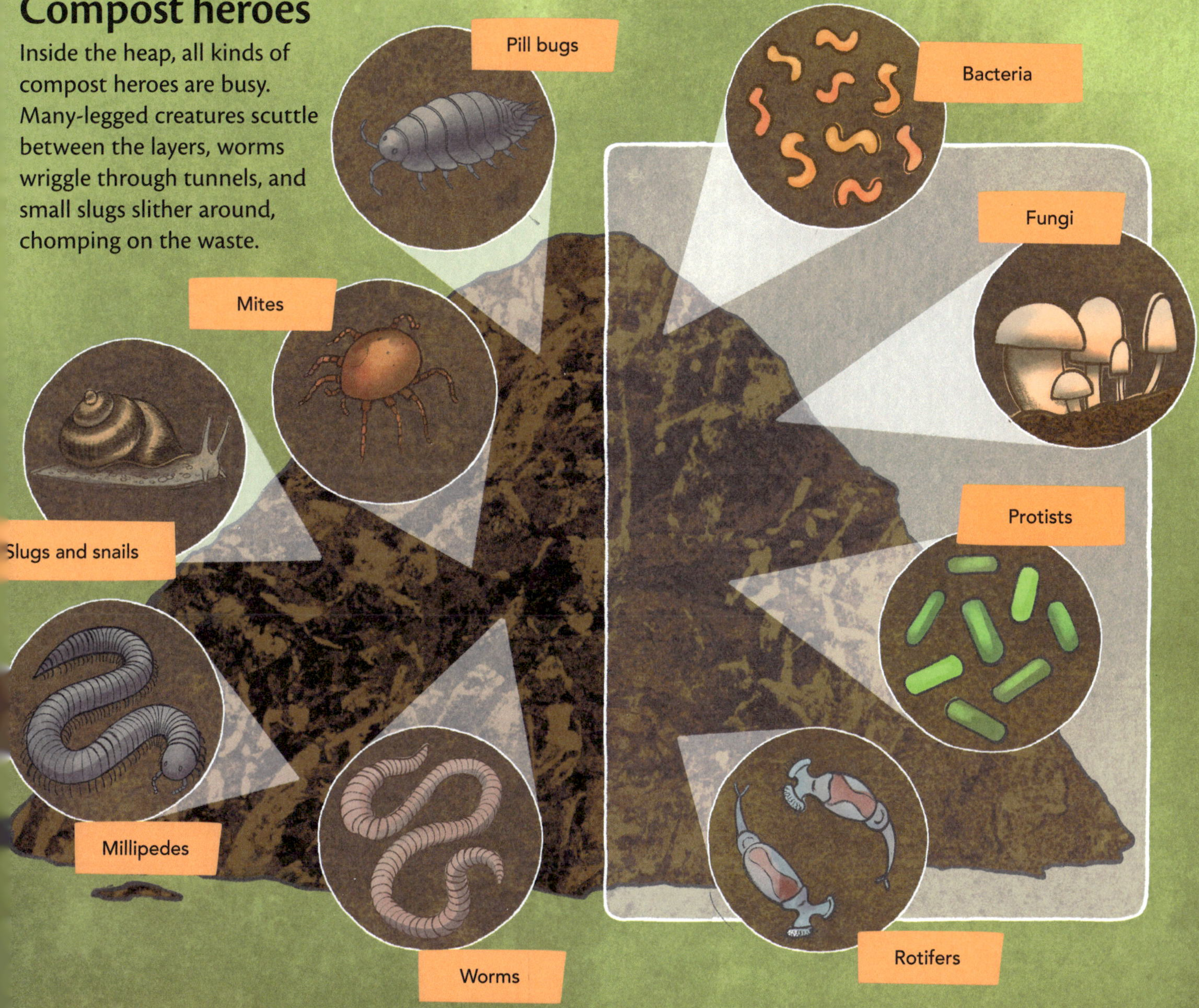

The compost is ready when it is **dark and crumbly and smells earthy**.

It can be **added to the soil** or to flowerpots.

It provides **nutrients**, **traps water and air**, and **contains healthy bacteria**.

Flowers will bloom, and **fruits and vegetables** will grow large and tasty.

Glossary

adaptations: changes to an animal's body that make it better suited to its environment.

amphibian: an animal—such as a frog, toad, or newt—that has smooth, damp skin, and can live on land and in water.

bacteria (plural of bacterium): a group of very tiny, very simple living things, found in almost every environment.

camouflage: body patterns, colors, and shapes that help hide animals in their natural environment.

carcass: the dead body of an animal.

carnivore: an animal that eats meat.

carrion: rotting meat.

chick: a young or newly hatched bird.

corals: tiny sea animals that have hard outer skeletons and live together in groups called colonies.

crustacean: an animal without a backbone that lives in the sea. Lobsters and crabs are examples of crustaceans.

decompose: to rot away.

decomposers: animals that help break down organic material, such as dead plants and animals.

detritus: dead organic material, such as dead plants and animals.

dissolve: when a solid mixes completely with a liquid, forming a solution.

ecosystem: a group of different types of organisms that interact with each other and the environment that they live in.

endangered: at risk of becoming extinct (dying out).

extinction: a species of plant or animal is extinct if there are no more living examples of it on the planet.

fungi (plural of fungus): a group of organisms that includes yeast, molds, truffles, toadstools, and mushrooms.

glutton: a very greedy eater.

habitat: the natural home where a plant, animal, or other organism is suited to living.

herbivore: an animal that eats plants.

insect: an animal—such as an ant or butterfly—that has six legs and three parts to its body.

invertebrate: an animal without a backbone, such as a spider, jellyfish, or snail.

keystone species: an organism that is very important to the ecosystem it lives in, even when there aren't very many of it there.

larvae (plural of larva): a larva, or grub, is the early form of an insect or animal before it changes into its adult form.

maggots: the larvae of flies, which often live in rotting plants or meat.

mammal: an animal that breathes air, grows hair or fur, and which feeds on its mother's milk when it is very young.

marrow: a soft, fatty substance found at the center of bones.

marsupial: a group of mammals where the young complete their development in a pouch on the mother's belly, not in the womb.

microbes: living things that are so tiny we cannot see them with the naked eye. They can only be seen using a microscope.

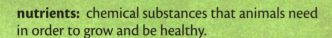

nutrients: chemical substances that animals need in order to grow and be healthy.

organism: a living thing.

parasite: a thing that lives on or in another animal or plant, and eats it for its food.

plumage: a bird's feathers, especially those that are long or brightly colored.

poaching: illegally hunting or catching animals.

predator: an animal that hunts and feeds on other animals.

prey: an animal that is hunted and eaten by another animal.

raucous: disturbingly loud.

reptile: an animal—such as a lizard, snake, or tortoise—that has scaly skin. Most reptiles lay eggs that have soft shells.

savanna: open grassland, with only a few trees.

scavenger: an animal that feeds on the remains of dead animals.

scrubland: an area of land where low shrubs, grasses, and herbs are the main types of vegetation.

sediment: a soft, wet substance at the bottom of a liquid, such as mud or sand.

serrated: objects that have a sawlike or jagged edge.

soil: the top layer of earth, which is usually made of rotten plant material, tiny pieces of rock, and clay.

species: a group of living things that have similar features or characteristics.

toxic: poisonous—harmful or unpleasant to those who touch or eat it.

vertebrate: an animal that has a skeleton and a backbone, or spine.

wetland: a marshy area of land, flooded with water for all or part of the year.

wingspan: the widest part of a bird's wings, measured across from wingtip to wingtip.